VGM Opportunities Series

D0530691

86B7 ✓

OPPORTUNITIES IN **ENVIRONMENTAL CAREERS**

Odom Fanning

Foreword by
Jay D. Hair, Ph.D.
President and Chief Executive Officer
National Wildlife Federation

VGM Career Horizons
a division of *NTC Publishing Group*
Lincolnwood, Illinois USA

Cover Photo Credits

Front cover: upper left, Allegheny College; upper right,
photo courtesy of Odom Fanning; lower left, West Virginia
University; lower right, University of Wisconsin–Stevens
Point, photo by Doug Moore.

Back cover: upper left, U.S. Fish and Wildlife Service;
upper right, Allegheny College; lower left, West Virginia
University; lower right, U.S. Fish and Wildlife Service.

Library of Congress Cataloging-in-Publication Data

Fanning, Odom.
   Opportunities in environmental careers / Odom Fanning ; foreword
by Jay D. Hair.

   ISBN 0-8442-8161-1 (hardbound) : $12.95. — ISBN 0-8442-8163-8
(softbound) : $9.95
     1. Environmental engineering—Vocational guidance.
2. Environmental protection—Vocational guidance.   3. Ecology-
-Vocational guidance.   I. Title.   II. Series.
TD156.F35   1991
363.7'0023'73—dc20   90-50734
                                                               CIP

1992 Printing

Published by VGM Career Horizons, a division of NTC Publishing Group.
© 1991 by NTC Publishing Group, 4255 West Touhy Avenue,
Lincolnwood (Chicago), Illinois 60646-1975 U.S.A.

   2 3 4 5 6 7 8 9 VP 9 8 7 6 5 4 3 2

ABOUT THE AUTHOR

Odom Fanning is a veteran free-lance science writer who has won numerous national awards for his environmental and medical writing. He was the first journalist to be presented the North American Association for Environmental Education's Citation of Merit for "his hallmark book *Opportunities in Environmental Careers.*" He also is contributing editor of *Internal Medicine World Report,* and he has authored a college textbook on environmental citizen action and a handbook on environmental management for developing countries.

A graduate of Emory University, Fanning was a science writer for the *Atlanta Journal* before becoming the first information officer for the Centers for Disease Control. He has been a newsletter publisher and a nationally syndicated columnist. On four occasions he was assigned to the White House—under four Presidents—as editor-in-chief of Presidential documents, including the *First Annual Report on Environmental Quality,* 1970.

Fanning is a Fellow of the American Association for the Advancement of Science and a member of the American Medical Writers Association, National Association of Science Writers, National Press Club, North American Association for Environmental Education, Society of Environmental Journalists, and Society of Professional Journalists.

PREFACE

It was a time of excitement and discovery, when the first edition of this book was published, on Earth Day in 1971. *Opportunities in Environmental Careers* predicted then that the next two decades would see enormous changes, among them that: The Congress would pass strong, new environmental laws and appropriate enormous sums for necessary programs; the federal and state governments would reorganize to implement them; business and industry would accommodate—even profit from—environmentally sound policies; colleges and universities would develop new, interdisciplinary environmental studies programs which would prove very attractive to students; and all these activities of the new environmental era would create unprecedented numbers of new jobs and challenges for young persons.

In a report marking its twentieth anniversary, the White House's Council on Environmental Quality recalls those days:

> That some people at the time doubted the long-term viability of the environmental movement is understandable given the national mood. . . . Moreover, the environmental movement in 1970 was demanding something that no nation had ever done before: the enactment of comprehensive, national legislation to protect the environment. Implicit in that goal . . . was a call for fundamental change in the American economic calculus. More and more people were beginning to appreciate clean air and clean water as precious resources that were neither free nor inexhaustible. Consequently, no person or business or community could appropriate those resources for their personal use to the detriment of others.[1]

---

[1]*Environmental Quality: The Twentieth Annual Report of the Council on Environmental Quality* (Washington, D.C.: U.S. Government Printing Office, 1990).

Since 1970 the population of the United States has grown by 22 percent, to over 250 million. The U.S. economy has grown more than three times as fast as its population. Its environmental problems have grown, and intensified. And the field of environmental management has grown, and changed, as well.

The Bureau of Labor Statistics has advanced a theory about the significance of generational turnover, especially in a rapidly growing field. Here is the way it works in environmental management: Within a few years of the first Earth Day, the older generation of environmentalists—environmental managers or professionals—of the 1960s retired and was replaced by a new generation. By the early 1990s, those environmentalists (no longer new but aging) were retiring, to be replaced by the second generation of *new environmentalists* (a term to be defined in Chapter 1). Each generation has been larger than the one before, measured in employment, which has grown from an estimated half million to one million, perhaps as large now as two million. A doubling every decade cannot long continue, but even with annual growth slowed to a low, single-digit percentage, the field of environmental management is sure to remain strong and viable well into the twenty-first century.

The decade 2000–2010 should see a third generation of new environmentalists assuming responsible positions in the workforce. Most of them were not even born at the time of the first Earth Day in 1970 and were still in secondary school at the time of the twentieth, in 1990.

Hence, for three reasons, this edition of *Opportunities in Environmental Careers* is directed precisely toward this emerging third generation of aspiring environmentalists. The first is to introduce the many career opportunities that lie ahead.

The second purpose is to explain a new concept in environmental management, the chain of "I's," which will be such a determinant of their future.

And a third is to describe the education necessary to qualify for an environmental career. The emphasis is on science and engineering as the principal tools for making environmental change. Beyond the purview of this book are the many arts—and some sciences—which also are necessary, such as economics, history, journalism, mediation, population, and statistics.

For each of two dozen major environmental professions this book examines such questions as:

- What education would you need to start a career?
- Where would you work?
- What would you earn?
- What is the job future?

The Council on Environmental Quality is optimistic, and so should we all be. It speaks a simple truth when it says:

> Americans believe strongly that environmental quality is an essential component of their long-term health and economic prosperity. Americans have demonstrated that they have the will to protect environmental quality and the capacity to act with energy, creativity, and a deep-seated sense of responsibility for future generations.

Odom Fanning
Bethesda, Maryland

FOREWORD

Virtually every public opinion survey on the environment in recent years has shown that the public ranks environmental protection among the most critical issues of our time. A recent poll by the National Wildlife Federation, conducted among undergraduate students nationally, showed an almost unanimous 95 percent agreeing that Congress should pass tougher laws to protect the environment. Ninety-four percent agreed that students can make a difference in environmental protection, and the same percentage of respondents said that they were personally willing to pay more for products that were environmentally safe.

Several years ago the National Wildlife Federation decided that it had an obligation to take stands on environmental issues broader than its traditional area, the conservation and enjoyment of wildlife. Since then, the Federation has been engaged in the frontlines of responsible environmental activism.

Our reasoning was simple: No nation can count on having abundant game, waterfowl, and fish *if* the forests are dying, *if* the protective atmospheric ozone layer is disappearing, and *if* climate shifts are causing droughts and coastal erosion. The heritage we hold dear includes all our natural resources.

An integral element of our program is support for a new national effort in environmental education. Consequently, I am privileged again to contribute a foreword to Odom Fanning's VGM Career Horizons guide to environmental education and careers.

This revised fifth edition has several features of note. One is the concept of the new environmentalism, employing interdisciplinary education, science, and management techniques directed towards advancing environmental quality and assuring a sustainable future.

Another is the book's emphasis on the sharing of hemispheric environmental problems and opportunities with neighboring nations, and its inclusion of outstanding interdisciplinary curricula in Canadian as well as U.S. universities. (I particularly appreciate this, having received my Ph.D. in zoology from the University of Alberta.)

And a third feature of this book is its recognition of the synergism that exists between the public and private sectors. It was such a recognition that led the Federation to establish, in 1982, a Corporate Conservation Council (CCC). The Council's purpose is to bring together conservationists and corporate executives from the corporate community to address environmental concerns of mutual and national interest.

One such concern is environmental education. Solving today's most pressing environmental problems and advancing the quality of the environment require a growing work force of well-trained scientists, engineers, technicians, and managers. To this end, the CCC is encouraging interdisciplinary environmental studies in our liberal arts colleges, universities, and graduate schools.

The Federation also backs efforts to raise the Environmental Protection Agency to the Cabinet level, making it a Department of Environmental Protection. Nearly all European countries already have such ministerial-level departments.

We want to see, by the year 2000, an environmentally literate society, a well-prepared work force, a strong economy that provides jobs and careers for all persons, and a continuing national and international commitment toward our environment and its natural resources. We are confident that environmental education is the optimum starting point for achieving these goals.

> Jay D. Hair, Ph.D.
> President and Chief Executive Officer
> National Wildlife Federation
> Washington, D.C.

DEDICATION

This edition is dedicated to Sarah Elaine and to Michael,
to all of their generation,
and to its environment.

CONTENTS

About the Author iii

Preface iv

Foreword vii

1.   The New Environmentalism 1

Catalysts for environmental change. The new
environmentalism. The chain of "I's." What types of
questions should you be able to answer after reading this
book?

2.   Education for the New Environmentalism 9

The new environmental colleges and universities.
Innovative liberal arts colleges. Major university
environmental programs. Environmental Education in
Canadian universities. Current stirrings.

3.   The Sciences of Living Things 27

Ecology. Biology. Environmental chemistry.

4.   Environmental Protection and Public Health 47

Current stirrings. "Healthy People 2000." Professionalism.
Environmental engineering. Environmental health sciences.
Environmental medicine (physicians, nurses, veterinarians).
Environmental sanitation. Health physics. Industrial
hygiene.

5. Natural Resources **89**

The Progressive Movement to the New Deal. Behind the
Modern Environment. Agricultural sciences. Fisheries
conservation. Forestry. Range management. Soil
conservation. Wildlife conservation.

6. Land Use and Human Settlements **117**

Trends in Land Use. Architecture. Geography. Landscape
architecture. Urban and regional planning.

7. Tomorrow's New Environmentalism **139**

Appendix A—Citizen Organizations **143**

Appendix B—Key Federal Agencies **145**

CHAPTER 1

THE NEW ENVIRONMENTALISM

> The Congress recognizes that each person should enjoy a healthful environment and that each person has a responsibility to contribute to the preservation and enhancement of the environment.—The National Environmental Policy Act of 1969.

Young persons today have known no other society than the one into which they were born and may take for granted what came before. They may not care much about tradition. Even the social revolutions of the 1960s and 1970s, which so drastically changed our society, may seem distant.

Our environmental heritage, like our social heritage, was established over many decades, by all citizens but especially be conservationists. One of the driving forces of the human rights movements of the 1960s was people's determination to establish permanent protection of many newly recognized environmental and consumer rights. The public interest law movement, epitomized by Ralph Nader, tied these two forces together; coalitions were formed involving both environmental and consumer rights with other groups, such as those promoting civil rights.

No one could be sure, at the beginning of the decade of the 1970s, how the human rights movement would turn out. Many young Americans were in revolt against misuse of government authority and particularly in turmoil over the devastation that was being inflicted on the American environment. The impact of the war in southeast Asia, and especially the effects of television coverage during this period, cannot be underestimated: people watched actual occurrences in Vietnam and were repelled by what they saw.

1

CATALYSTS FOR ENVIRONMENTAL CHANGE

Silent Spring, a book by Rachel Carson published in 1962, drama-
tized the price society pays for the indiscriminate use of technological
advances. Carson's thesis was that "we have allowed these chemicals
[pesticides] to be used with little or no investigation of their effect on
soil, water, wildlife, and man himself. Future generations are unlikely
to condone our lack of prudent concern for the integrity of the natural
world that supports all life." *Silent Spring* galvanized public opinion
for the environmental changes to come.

Young persons, in particular, became aroused over pollution, blight,
deterioration, waste, and destruction of our natural valuables, and over
the terrible hurt to everybody's health. Late in the 1960s, the media
began to catalyze public opinion behind a change in political policies.
Then, on January 28, 1969, a gigantic oil spill occurred offshore at
Santa Barbara, California. The television pictures of seabirds, their
feathers coated with oily gunk, suffering and dying while people who
cared tried to rescue them, symbolized all forms of technology's conflict with the environment. Capturing the national attention, that single
event provoked the public into action.

The public health movement was two and one-half centuries old, and
the conservation movement one century old, at the time. Environmental
stewardship was entrenched in our American value system. But most
observers credit that catastrophe on the California coast with marking
the start of the *new* environmental era. Modest organization work to
promote the cause of the environment continued for the next year. Then,
the following April of 1970, an estimated twenty million Americans
participated in the first Earth Day, a more-or-less spontaneous, unex-
pectedly successful celebration.

Concurrently, a great deal of political groundwork was being laid.
Through a rare combination of imagination, political leadership, and
chance, the Congress produced a gem of a law in the National Environmental Policy Act of 1969 (NEPA). It was full enough of rhetoric to
satisfy the most ardent Earth Day demonstrator. Every law has its
rhetoric, but NEPA had more: a strong action-forcing device. Its Section
102(2)(c) requires an environmental impact statement in advance of any
federal action that might significantly affect the quality of the environ-

ment. This requirement has revolutionized U.S., even international, decision making. It asks governmental agencies: "Wait! Do we know all we should know about what you propose to do? Do we understand its consequences? Can we make it safer for people and more benign for the environment? Do the benefits outweigh the costs?"

If such questions had been asked—and if the technology had existed to answer them—Los Angeles might have been built so as to minimize its smog and traffic congestion. The automobile might have been developed so as to avoid harmful emissions. Certainly hazardous and toxic chemicals would not have been dumped in thousands of locations, from which they provably cause illness, and probably cause much of the rising incidence of cancer, miscarriages, birth defects, mental retardation, and other serious threats to health and life.

We may not be able to do much about the chemical estate we have inherited from previous generations. But we can unburden future generations by not making similar mistakes in our own uses of technology. The major social movement which offers the potential for stepping back, taking a second look, and making more rational social, political, and technological decisions is what we call the *new environmentalism.*

THE NEW ENVIRONMENTALISM

The new environmentalism has three facets: education, science, and management. It employs them in new ways. It is ends-oriented, not means-oriented. Contrast the old with the new as follows:

Education   It might seem that defining *environmental education* would be simple and as straightforward as defining "medical education" or "engineering education," but such is not the case. One authority is Dr. John F. Disinger, associate director for environmental education at the ERIC Clearinghouse for Science, Mathematics, and Environmental Education at Ohio State University. In a paper published in 1983 titled "Environmental Education's Definitional Problem," he traced the term's roots back to the early 1900s nature study and conservation and outdoor education. Despite the years of discussion since then, evidenced by more than fifty references in the paper, Dr. Disinger concluded that there was no consensus on a definition of environmental education.

A major problem in defining environmental education, compared to other types of education, is that it is all-encompassing. The difficulty begins with the environment's not being a discipline. Medical education is education *in* medicine. Engineering education is *in* engineering, and so forth throughout scores of disciplines. But environmental education is education *about* the environment.

Whatever definition is attempted must rationalize that dilemma. It must apply to both formal and nonformal education, to professional as well as nonprofessional, to vocational and general, and to all ages.

However, the need for a definition of environmental education is widely recognized, and attempts at consensus are being made by a number of organizations. One effort has been under way since 1989 and is being coordinated by the American Society for Testing and Materials (ASTM, described in Chapter 2). Its consensus process is expected to lead eventually to a new set of standards for environmental education. These standards would include, as a central feature, a definition. The committee and its task forces are confronted by a list of fifty-six issues under the categories of (a) awareness, (b) knowledge, (c) skills, (d) attitudes, and (e) participation.

ASTM has "accepted," as the best definition so far available, the criteria—still not a definition—internationally agreed upon at the 1977 United Nations (Unesco-UNEP) Intergovernmental Conference on Environmental Education held at Tbilisi, Georgia, U.S.S.R. There it was agreed that the basic aim of environmental education is

...to succeed in making individuals and communities *understand* the complex nature of the natural and built environments resulting from the interaction of their physical, biological, social, economic, and cultural aspects, and *acquire* the knowledge, values, attitudes, and practical skills to participate in a responsible and effective way in anticipating and solving environmental problems, and in the management of the quality of the environment. [Italics added.]

The North American Association for Environmental Education (NAAEE is also described in Chapter 2), organized in 1971, has never defined its field, either. NAAEE is organized into three membership sections: elementary and secondary education, nonformal education, and environmental studies. In 1990 testimony before the U.S. Senate's Committee on Environmental and Public Works, an NAAEE representative described environmental education as incorporating ten elements. They include: (a) integrating knowledge from disciplines across the natural sciences, social sciences, and humanities; (b) relating environmental knowledge, problem-solving, values, and sensitivity at every level; and (c) emphasizing the role of values, morality, and ethics in shaping attitudes and actions affecting the environment.

Until ASTM or NAAEE—separately or together—come up with an agreed-upon definition, environmental education will continue to have a definitional problem. In the following pages, especially in Chapter 2, this book deals with higher education designed to prepare graduates to perform professional duties in the application of science and technology to the protection of the human environment or the preservation and use of natural resources.

Science　The new environmentalism also embraces environmental science. Traditionally, scientists and engineers worked on narrow disciplinary problems such as those having to do with climate, air turbulence, estuaries, forests, epidemics, earthquakes, and groundwater, to name a few. After 1970, environmental scientists broadened their perspective in response to governmental support for interdisciplinary research and development.

There was probably another subtle reason for this broadening, too. New technology such as high-speed computers relieved scientists of much of the drudgery which long had characterized their work. Machines could handle vast amounts of data with the speed of light. Scientists could devote their time to things that were more "fun," one of which was interacting with fellow scientists in a teamwork approach to more broad-based environmental problems. For the first time, they could think in terms of "managing" or manipulating environmental phenomena, as easily as they could conduct scientific experiments in the laboratory.

Management　Environmental management is an action term, which refers to all activities, public and private, undertaken to achieve the goals of environmental quality. In such activities lie many jobs and careers. This is the author's definition:

> Environmental management is an interdisciplinary, integrated effort, involved with the very fabric of people's lives, focused on interrelated environmental problems and employing the findings of science, the techniques of engineering, and the understanding of the social sciences to preserve the human environment, to utilize natural resources, and to better society.

THE CHAIN OF "I's"

Note, in the definition, the "chain of I's": *interdisciplinary/integrated/involved*. Take each link:

Interdisciplinary.   Whereas once it was thought sufficient for disciplines to stand alone, the sciences—especially the natural sciences and their forms of application as in engineering and technology—now are recognized as closely interconnected. Biology, chemistry, ecology, physics, and other scientific disciplines, linked as in a chain, must be employed together in the solution of complex environmental problems. That is why we speak of many fields, including environmental management, as interdisciplinary.

Integrated means a part incorporated into a larger whole. To the sciences must be added such other disciplines as engineering, business management and public administration, communications, economics, education, the humanities, law, philosophy, political science, sales and marketing, and the social sciences. Environmental management is an integrated form of interdisciplinary endeavor.

Involved means that environmental management endeavors, while interdisciplinary and integrated, must be undertaken with the full appreciation that they are focused on the human environment, therefore people are affected. For this reason, environmental managers must themselves be involved in the broader society; they must be good environmental citizens, whether or not their profession has a code of ethics, requires a license, or confers a title such as Doctor. Some of the ways in which this citizen involvement occurs are to be found throughout the chapters to follow.

WHAT QUESTIONS SHOULD YOU BE ABLE TO ANSWER AFTER READING THIS BOOK?

1. What type of college or university would you prefer to attend, and are you likely to find a suitable environmental studies curriculum there?
2. What are some environmental fields you could enter with the bachelor's degree?
3. Biotechnology is an emerging area of the biological sciences. What disciplines contribute to biotechnology? What are some of its applications, and why is it a viable career option?
4. What is ecology and what do ecologists do?
5. What is the significance of conservation biology?
6. Why does one professor call a degree in environmental chemistry "a ticket to a career in business, sales, journalism, or law"?
7. What are the advantages to alternate periods of work and college study?
8. What are some of the opportunities for environmental engineers overseas?
9. What are some of the national health objectives for the year 2000? How does success in meeting them depend upon adequate supplies of environmental health scientists and other workers, and what kinds of workers?
10. Why do some conservation fields now substitute the noun *management* for *conservationist?*
11. Why is agricultural science considered an environmental field?
12. Why do the states grant licenses to some environmental professionals and not to others?

CHAPTER 2

EDUCATION FOR THE NEW ENVIRONMENTALISM

Today, no self-respecting campus is without some gesture toward environmentalism, and the more substantive enterprises represent a major departure in university focus and format toward interdisciplinary, multi-function, problem-oriented teaching, research, and outreach.— Clay Schoenfeld and John F. Disinger.

If you are college-bound, your choice of college may be determined by finances, geographic preference, class grades and SATs, the institution's reputation, its rating in various directories, and other factors, subjective as well as objective (including perhaps where your parents went to college).

It is unwise, even for the student highly motivated toward an environmental career, to focus too early on only one institution or type. You can get a good grounding in science and the liberal arts at almost any of the 1,200 community colleges or 1,800 four-year colleges and universities in America. Among the important factors is finding a school at which you feel comfortable but challenged. Many students transfer, especially between sophomore and junior years, so an initial choice can easily be changed, usually without significant loss of credits.

This chapter is focused on environmental studies (sometimes abbreviated ES). This is a type of higher education that is *interdisciplinary/integrated/involved*. A bachelor's degree in ES may qualify one for entry to some fields for which the bachelor's degree is standard for professional practice, e.g., agricultural sciences, fisheries, soils or

9

wildlife conservation, and range management. Even in the field of environmental health, there are some professions, e.g., industrial hygiene, and several categorial specialties in which a postgraduate degree may not be necessary.

Furthermore, there are new functions which the environmental studies graduate may be better qualified to perform than someone who has a narrow science or engineering specialty. An example may be preparing environmental impact studies and statements or editing and publishing scientific, engineering, or economic reports. A good grounding in English and social science, beneficial to any professional, would be especially so in this work.

The College Board's *Index of Majors* lists more than 350 colleges and universities offering bachelor's degrees in environmental design, environmental health engineering, or—in more than 250 cases—environmental science or studies. Many of these institutions were surveyed and asked to comment on the success of their programs and to supply literature such as catalogs. Following is a selection from their responses.

THE NEW ENVIRONMENTAL COLLEGES
AND UNIVERSITIES

Most of the dozen or so new environmental colleges established in the late 1960s or early 1970s in response to rising environmental interest are thriving. Some started "from scratch." Others were established as units within existing liberal arts colleges or universities. These new institutions offer unique opportunities for satisfaction, inspiration, idealism, pragmatism, enjoyment, and involvement in real-life problems. Many of the professors are themselves products of the new environmentalism, and generally they are dedicated to teaching. Students, by and large, have a deep and sincere interest in environmental affairs.

College of the Atlantic is a small (only two hundred students), private, coeducational institution which occupies a 26-acre shorefront campus on beautiful Mount Desert Island at Bar Harbor, Maine. COA (as it is abbreviated) dates from 1972. It offers three "resource areas":

environmental science, human studies, and art and design. Thirty-six credits are required for graduation, plus an essay in human ecology, a one-term workshop stressing problem-solving, laboratory or field work, internship for up to one year, and completion of a final project leading to the Bachelor of Arts in Human Ecology.

The Evergreen State College, Olympia, Washington, opened in 1971 with a number of new ideas. The major one is a focus on full-time interdisciplinary study, with environmental studies as a core program.

Other innovations are group contracts, individual contracts, internships, and part-time courses. All of this is to be found in its own exceptional environment: a 1,000-acre, forested campus bordering waters of Eld Inlet on Puget Sound and new buildings that have been praised by architectural critics.

In addition to ES, Evergreen offers four-year curricula in ecological agriculture, energy systems, and marine studies. In 1984 Evergreen began a Master of Environmental Studies program as well.

Also in Washington State, **Huxley College of Environmental Studies** is one of three cluster units of Western Washington University at Bellingham, a major institution with over 9,000 students, about 300 of whom are enrolled in Huxley. This college-within-a-college is named for Thomas Henry Huxley, the father of the eminent British family of scientists and writers. It is primarily an upper-division institution; transfers with good academic records are welcome for junior-year standing. Concentrations (majors) include human ecology, marine resources, marine planning, education, administration, systems and simulations, analysis, health, and monitoring. From 56 to 80 credit hours are required for the bachelor of science or bachelor of arts degrees.

At the undergraduate level, three of Huxley's academic majors—environmental science, environmental policy and assessment, and environmental education—lead to the bachelor of science degree. A fourth major, environmental studies, leads to the bachelor of arts. There are a number of cooperative majors leading to both degrees. For example, there is a strong program in environmental journalism and writing directed by a distinguished conservation writer, Michael Frome.

The ES program of **New College of the University of South Florida,** Sarasota, is described by its coordinator (in an ecological metaphor) as having.

> . . . achieved a good measure of success, continuity, and momentum; yet in many ways ours is still a year-to-year existence as we scurry about like early mammals trying to find our niche. We have survived and thrived not because we have fulfilled our ultimate potential, but because we have been resilient enough to bounce back from potentially lethal situations.

New College opened its doors in 1964 and graduated its first class in 1967. Its ES program was inaugurated in 1972. The program's first crisis coincided with a crisis for the college itself: Faculty status was denied the environmentalists, many resigned, and simultaneously New College almost failed, only to be saved by a merger with the University of South Florida.

Seniors must prepare research proposals, on which the college attempts to procure funding. More than 100 have been completed. One senior thesis led to a gift to the college of a 123-acre bayfront tract for ES research. Many of the studies relate to land- and water-use problems peculiar to South Florida.

In 1963, a conference sponsored by the Ford Foundation and held in Phoenix, Arizona, challenged one hundred leading educators, business people, and scientists to design an "ideal college of the 21st century." Alan Weisman describes it in *Arizona Highways* for March 1990:

> In the model they envisioned, students would not merely sit in classrooms reading about someone else's experiences but would spend up to half their time in the field in direct contact with their subjects. The notion was so fascinating that within three years a group of the original conferees founded just such an institution on a breezy 620-acre campus north of Prescott.

For seven or eight years, **Prescott College** attracted international attention. Then the dream ended, according to Weisman:

> But in their zeal to turn their concept into reality, the college authorities did not foresee the rising interest rates that steadily pushed mortgage payments on the new campus beyond reach. As debts outstripped resources and income, the school faced bankruptcy. Just before Christmas

that year [1974], the Prescott community was shocked to learn that the college must close.

The college community could not accept defeat: Teachers taught without salary, classes were held outdoors, and thirty students came back without expectation of acceptable credits or degrees. With grit, the community gradually rebuilt the college. Finally, in 1984, the regional association re-awarded Prescott College accreditation at the highest level; this is believed to be the only time that such an academic resurrection has occurred in the United States, writes Weisman.

Today, Prescott College is established and thriving, with a modest campus in the town of Prescott, in the mile-high forested mountains of central Arizona. By the end of the decade, there are expected to be about five hundred resident students, with about the same number in the adult degree program and graduate studies.

Environmental studies is central to Prescott's philosophy of helping people "to thrive in and enhance our world ecology." The areas of concentration include natural history, human ecology, environmental education and interpretation, and environmental conservation.

Beginning with wilderness orientation, students are introduced to a variety of physical, social, and cultural conditions. Advanced students lead newcomers on an expedition to an area such as the Grand Canyon for up to nineteen days of backpacking. Independent studies and internships take students to Colorado for alpine ecology, Mexico for cultural ecology, and Costa Rica for tropical ecology. In 1968, Prescott College established the Center for Indian Bilingual Teacher Training to produce teacher aides with two years of college. Its purposes are to increase the proportion of certified American Indian teachers and to counterbalance the high failure rate of Indian students.

Simon's Rock of Bard College, Great Barrington, Massachusetts, is unique in that it accepts high school students after completion of the ninth, tenth, or eleventh grade as well as high school graduates. There are special programs to assist the younger students in making the transition to college. Simon's Rock graduates typically earn the B.A. at age 19 or 20, essentially having skipped the last two years of high school.

ES is an interdisciplinary major. It consists of a core sequence of courses combined with a concentration in natural science or social science.

Internships are available at several locations, one being Nicosia, Cyprus. Students with junior status have the option of spending their third year at one of four cooperating universities.

INNOVATIVE LIBERAL ARTS COLLEGES

The liberal arts college generally is constituted of a community of scholars devoted to teaching (and limited research and consulting); largely dedicated students; and, often, a rural or small-town atmosphere free of the distractions of the city. Virtually every such college has arrangements with several universities whereby you can transfer at, say, the end of the junior year to a university school of forestry, engineering, law, or other professional school. Then, after completing one year in the professional school, you would receive a bachelor's degree from the first college and, ultimately, the professional degree from the university.

Here is a selection of smaller institutions whose environmental programs—perhaps whose total approach to liberal arts education—can be called innovative:

Allegheny College at Meadville, Pennsylvania, sixty miles north of Pittsburgh, is one of the few liberal arts colleges to have a full-fledged environmental science department. It is an outgrowth of an aquatic environments major dating from 1971 and an environmental resource management major begun in 1977. Bachelor's degrees are offered in aquatic environments—which has a strong groundwater component—and in environmental studies, emphasizing social science applications. Both interdisciplinary ES majors share a core of courses in environmental science, biology, geology, mathematics, political science, economics, and chemistry. Independent study and internships are offered. Five miles from the campus is a college-owned, 283-acre natural area used for ecological and environmental research.

Cooperative programs are offered wherein students spend three years at Allegheny and two years in environmental management or forestry at

Duke University or the University of Michigan leading to the bachelor's and master's degrees. Such programs are increasingly being offered jointly by colleges and universities which otherwise have no connection.

At **Oberlin College,** Oberlin, Ohio, ES is presented as interdisciplinary study of human interactions with natural and social environments. A second major in a science is strongly recommended. Of central concern is the impact of technology on natural environments and the implications of this impact for human welfare. The program seeks to apply the perspectives of the humanities, social sciences, biology, and the physical sciences to environmental and natural resource issues. Students are prepared for graduate work and careers in the environmental sciences, law, public health, public policy, or public administration.

At **St. Lawrence University** at Canton, New York, the ES major may combine environmental studies with biology, economics, geology, government, psychology, or sociology for a combined major. Many courses focus on rural environmental problems, taking maximum advantage of the university's setting.

Located in the heart of the Blue Ridge Mountains ten miles from Asheville, North Carolina, at Swannanoa, **Warren Wilson College** has a century-long heritage of service to Appalachia. This small, private college—it has only 500 students—started its environmental studies program in 1977. In recent years, ES has been the second-largest major on campus, with sixty to seventy students enrolled at all times!

This is not a school for effete city dwellers; the atmosphere is rural, and the campus includes a working farm. Each student, to graduate, must complete sixty hours of community service. Most students earn much of their room and board by working fifteen hours per week on one of the more than sixty work crews on campus tasks—raising hogs or broccoli, plowing the fields, building sheds or walls, or clerical or janitorial tasks among them. An ES major involves disciplinary breadth, depth in a concentration selected and designed by the student, and field and laboratory experience. Most students complete two internships.

Outreach projects address local, regional, national, and international environmental needs. Twice a year students, faculty, and staff help coordinate and participate in stream cleanups. Warren Wilson teams also are conducting feasibility studies of alternate crops for Appalachian farmers. On a number of visits to a Caribbean country, work crews have built a school and a clinic.

MAJOR UNIVERSITY ENVIRONMENTAL PROGRAMS

Disciplinary environmental studies originated with the establishment of the land-grant colleges and universities in the mid-nineteenth century. Frequently called "agricultural and mechanical" colleges, they offered agriculture, animal husbandry, engineering, home economics, nutrition, and other applied arts and sciences. They generally came later than two other types of state institutions: teachers' colleges and state universities. The latter emphasized at their establishment, and still do, liberal arts plus such professional schools as law, medicine, and business administration.

At several major universities, the comprehensive undergraduate and graduate ES programs are so diverse as to be breath-taking. At **Ohio State University,** Columbus, for example, the School of Natural Resources offers twenty-six options in seven major environmental fields. At **Washington State University** at Pullman, the faculty resource list includes ninety members representing over forty disciplines. And at the **University of Wisconsin-Madison,** seventy faculty from twenty-six departments contribute to the graduate degree programs and (to some extent) to the curriculum for a certificate in ES accompanying a bachelor's degree.

For the student who prefers a large-university atmosphere, with such advantages as library and laboratory facilities unavailable elsewhere as well as contact with research scientists and possibly industry managers who are potential employers, these are the places to go.

The further diversity of large universities is suggested in this brief selection:

At **California State University, Hayward,** ES is combined with geography, but the course offerings cover a wide range of natural and social sciences: anthropology, biology, geology, etc.

The **University of the District of Columbia,** Washington, D.C., offers (on its modern, but decidedly inland, metropolitan campus) a baccalaureate degree in ES with a marine science major. Added to the usual arts and sciences are biological, physical, and geological ocean-ography; marine instrumentation; statistics, computer science, and mathematics. With support from the Environmental Protection Agency, the National Oceanic and Atmospheric Administration, the Smithsonian Institution, and other agencies, students are offered unexcelled hiring opportunities and on-the-job training, including summer cruises and scuba diving.

Suffolk County, New York, at the east end of Long Island, has adopted an Environmental Bill of Rights to preserve its vacation-retreat, marine environment. In this attractive setting, **Long Island University, South-ampton Campus** (the town's name is Southampton) specializes in assisting local citizens and governments by training specialists in envi-ronmental science and environmental studies focused on indigenous marine problems. (Graduates find jobs far afield, of course, as well as locally.) A unique concentration called appropriate technology is fo-cused on the study of solar, wind, and other renewable energy sources.

Tufts University, at Medford, Massachusetts, has an ES program, based in the Department of Biology, offered as a co-major only with enrollment in another undergraduate major field. Tufts also has estab-lished the Environmental Literacy Institute—the first of its kind—with the objective of training faculty to integrate environmental subjects into virtually all undergraduate and graduate courses. Two major corpora-tions and the Environmental Protection Agency are funding the pilot program, whose findings and materials will be made available to other colleges and universities.

Since 1972 the **University of Vermont** at Burlington has offered a special university-wide undergraduate curricular option in ES which has been quite successful. Some 350 students are enrolled. Faculty members' ties to political leaders—in the community, the state, and Washington, D.C.—extend their influence beyond that of the idyllic Green Mountain setting (and beyond that of many larger universities). At any time, faculty also are engaged in foreign travel because of their involvement in international environmental affairs. Undergraduate stu-dents benefit from these activities, and to some extent have the oppor-tunity to participate in them.

The **University of Wisconsin/Stevens Point** dates its highly regarded undergraduate program in natural resources from 1946. It may be both the oldest ES program in the nation and the largest, with fourteen hundred undergraduates in forestry, resource management, water resources, soil science, wildlife, and paper science. Overall, about 85 percent of its bachelor's graduates immediately find jobs in their fields or go to graduate school.

Yale University at New Haven, Connecticut, bases its small ES program, called "Studies in the Environment," in the Department of History and offers it only as a second major together with one in another department. While there are no prerequisites, the thirteen term courses must include certain specific sciences, according to a distribution plan, and there must be a senior project and colloquium.

The **State University of New York College of Environmental Science and Forestry** at Syracuse is both old and new, small and large. CESF was chartered in 1911 as a school of forestry and rechartered in 1972. It boasts a small-college atmosphere with only sixteen hundred students and a typical class size of twelve, yet is affiliated with neighboring Syracuse University, which provides the academic, cultural, and social benefits of a large campus. Costs are low, standards high.

CESF offers only environmentally related programs and focuses on upper division and graduate education.

The advanced early admission program is designed for high school students who are strongly motivated toward entering such a program after two years elsewhere. The first two years of college may be taken at any of fifty-four approved institutions in New York and seven other states.

CESF is comprised of schools of biology, chemistry, and ecology; environmental and resource engineering; forestry; and landscape architecture. One program, the forest technician curriculum, is designed to allow its graduates immediate job entry at the technician level. All the other programs lead to the bachelor's degree (or higher).

The Bachelor of Science in Environmental Studies (BS/ES) is offered in the School of Landscape Architecture, which should not put anyone off as it has broader horizons. Approximately one hundred upper-division undergraduates are enrolled.

Students typically enter the BS/ES program with sixty-two lower-division credits. During junior and senior years, they are required to complete a group of core courses in the humanities, natural sciences, and social sciences. But each student's program is flexible and is worked out with advisors to meet individual career goals. The BS/ES degree is granted at the end of four years as an undergraduate (two at CESF) and the successful completion of 125 credit hours.

A dual curriculum leading to a bachelor's degree also is offered in environmental and forest biology and resources management.

Master's degrees are offered in all areas of specialization, as are doctorates. Emphasis in these postgraduate curricula is on administration, policy, planning, and regulations—in six areas of concentration: energy, land use, water resources, urban ecosystems, waste management, and environmental communication.

ENVIRONMENTAL EDUCATION IN CANADIAN UNIVERSITIES

The United States' *First Annual Report on Environmental Quality,* 1970, described the past and presaged the future:

> Cooperation between the United States and Canada on environmental problems has a long history. Their joint attention is now focused on the Great Lakes, St. Lawrence River water boundary, and on the Arctic region. U.S.-Canada agreements on the Great Lakes go back to the Boundary Waters Treaty of 1906. The Great Lakes is the largest fresh water body in the world. Most of the population of Canada and much of that of the United States lives near its borders, and pollution of the Great Lakes concerns both nations. The intergovernmental body chiefly responsible is the International Joint Commission of the United States and Canada.

By the early 1990s, there was a long list of agreements between the U.S. and Canada. These pledge the two sovereign nations, among other things, to (a) restore and maintain the chemical, physical, and biological integrity of the Great Lakes Basin ecosystem; (b) cooperate, along the border, in dealing with accidental releases of pollutants which may cause damage and constitute a threat to public health, property, or welfare; (c) control the export, import, and transit across the border of hazardous wastes, whether for treatment, storage, or disposal; and (d) restore the North American continent's waterfowl populations to the levels of the early 1970s.

No source of international friction between two friendly neighbors is more exasperating than the problem of fallout from acid rain. Much of this type of air pollution originates in the United States from industry and power generation but falls in Canada due to atmospheric patterns.

Despite U.S. measures to reduce acidifying emissions through the Clean Air Act Amendments of 1977, Canada continued to object; the resulting acid rain was exceeding the absorptive capacity of Canadian lakes and forests, killing fish and wildlife and denuding trees and undergrowth. In 1980 the U.S. Congress passed legislation establishing a ten-year acid rain research program.

A decade later, the problem remaining, Congress wrote into the Clean Air Act Amendments of 1990 more stringent mandates that would cut acidic air pollutants by nearly half.

The two countries share not only the same environment and the same values, but also the same commitment to environmental education at all levels. In the early 1990s, both countries' top legislative bodies were, at the same time, considering ways to bolster environmental education. The Environment Ministers from the ten provinces call theirs the "Green Plan." Among the things called for is the integration of environmental education into all areas of learning. The goal is environmental literacy for the entire population.

Canada's major universities were ready. **Simon Fraser University** at Burnaby, British Columbia, traces its origins to the post-war (World War II) baby boom. The first students graduated in 1968. Today, this is a distinguished institution of higher learning, with approximately fifteen thousand students in five faculties.

Citizens of the United States may know Simon Fraser University best for its beautiful campus atop a 1,200-foot mountain, with a series of multi-million-dollar concrete buildings which have won international design awards for Canadian architects Arthur Erickson and Geoffrey Massey. Ecology is one of three "streams" (we might call them tracks) in biological science. Simon Fraser offers graduate programs in environmental toxicology, natural resources management, and other environmental areas. The Canadian government, and Canadian industry, generously fund research and scholarships. According to a recent survey, many natural resources graduates are working in consulting, government, industry, or teaching, mostly in Canada but to some extent in the United States and elsewhere.

In the same province is found another strong ES program, that of the **University of Victoria.** Students are required to combine ES with a traditional discipline. This second major might be, for example, in economics, geography, or biology. Major areas of specialty are resource management, environmental planning, environmental protection, and environmental journalism.

At the **University of Waterloo,** Ontario, Man-Environment Studies were initiated in 1969. Now called Environment and Resource Studies, it is a four-year honors program leading to a bachelor of environmental studies degree. The faculty is drawn from geography, architecture, and urban and regional planning. A theme since its early years has been the balanced relationship that should exist between environment and development. Out of nationwide discussions (not just on campuses, and not just regarding education), there evolved the concept of environmentally sustainable development with the crucial ecological and equity issues entailed. Advanced teaching methods are used, such as case study analyses, role playing simulations of environmental disputes, and small-group assignments to task achievement.

ENVIRONMENTAL EDUCATION: CURRENT STIRRINGS

Recognizing the rapid expansion of environmental activity in Canada, several years ago the U.S. National Association for Environmental Education, founded in 1971, changed its name to the **North American Association for Environmental Education** (NAAEE). Since the mid-1980s the association's total membership has grown (in both the U.S. and Canada); currently three of the twenty-three members of its board of directors are Canadians; its annual meetings attract twice the number of five years earlier; its publications list has grown into a small catalog; and its bimonthly *Environmental Communicator* has expanded from a newsletter into a respectable magazine. Among its regular features is a listing of job and internship openings. Association representatives represent the field of environmental education at international conferences and testify before congressional hearings (as noted in Chapter 1). NAAEE is the leading membership organization for anyone engaged in environmental education, formal or nonformal.

The U.S. Department of Education, through its National Institute of Education, sponsors clearinghouses—called ERICs, for Educational Resources Information Centers—in a number of subject areas. Environmental education is grouped with two others in the **ERIC Clearinghouse for Science, Mathematics, and Environmental Education,** located at Ohio State University, Columbus. Since 1972, this center has been a focal point for editing, publishing, and distributing environmental education books and other materials for teachers and other professionals. For over a decade it published the NAAEE's proceedings and monographs. Its data base probably stores more information on environmental education than any other library in the world. Bulletins and publications lists are available to anyone.

The Alliance for Environmental Education (AEE) is a coalition of industry and membership organizations formed in 1972 "to dramatically broaden the base of citizens who can make informed judgments about environmental issues." Environmental outreach centers are being established at one hundred or more colleges and universities and other institutions, such as outdoor education centers. They are designed to serve schools and the public with environmental education services— something like agricultural extension services. Although there are no individual memberships in AEE, it is a valuable source of information as to what is going on in environmental education, and anyone can subscribe to its bimonthly newspaper, *Network Exchange.*

The **American Society for Testing and Materials** (ASTM), based in Philadelphia, is a voluntary consensus organization. (Consensus means reaching general agreements; it is the process by which it was determined that a plank would be two inches by four inches, to use a simple example.) Over the years ASTM has developed more than one hundred widely accepted criteria and standards, mostly for manufactured products. ASTM's reputation was made by its success in dealing with tangibles; a recent standard developed through ASTM is for recycled paper, so it is not unfamiliar with recycling, a major environmental issue. Its first venture into intangibles was the development of a standard for emergency medical services.

Since 1989, ASTM has been engaged in a consensus-development project in environmental education; defining the term, mentioned in Chapter 1, is only the beginning. Developing a new set of voluntary standards is the objective of this project, which is funded by government (the U.S. Environmental Protection Agency and the Federal Interagency Committee on Education's Subcommittee on Environmental Education), industry (the Alliance for Environmental Education), and perhaps philanthropic foundations. A large committee and several subcommittees have been organized and are meeting to consider environmental literacy, formal education, nonformal education and communication, and technical training. Anyone interested is welcome to attend these meetings, and working papers are available.

In 1990 the Congress recognized that the solution of environmental problems requires "a well-educated and trained, professional work force," and passed the National Environmental Education Act. When signed by President Bush, it established as the policy of the United States a federal mandate to "support a program of education on the environment." A new Office of Environmental Education in the U.S. Environmental Protection Agency is responsible for teacher training, internships and fellowships, awards in recognition of outstanding contributions to environmental education, and many other activities, including teacher exchanges between the United States, Canada, and Mexico.

The CEIP Fund, Inc.—a private, nonprofit organization, formerly the Center for Environmental Intern Programs—is based in Boston and has five regional offices. Established in 1972, CEIP is the nation's largest on-the-job trainer for environmental careers, with an annual budget of more than \$4 million. Each year the center places more than three hundred college students and recent graduates in short-term, paid professional-level positions with corporations, consulting firms, government agencies, and nonprofit organizations. The normal span is twenty weeks, and median weekly salaries average over $360. At the completion of a project, a CEIP associate (as a participant is called) usually returns to college or goes on to graduate school. The majority of CEIP projects are in water quality, environmental health and safety, species protection, and the management and protection of wetlands and open space. A newsletter, *Connections,* is published, and books and reports are available on this and other CEIP programs.

Environmental career services is a second effort, which involves publications and activities such as conferences concerned with environmental careers. CEIP sponsors an annual national environmental careers conference and publishes the proceedings as a paperback book.

CEIP also is conducting a five-year effort to increase the diversification of the environmental work force. Says a CEIP publication:

> The environmental profession will experience a labor shortage [by the year 2000], as will other career fields. With the rapid demographic changes and the expansion of the environmental field, there must be changes in the human resource approach of employers, particularly in attracting and retaining minorities and women. Since the environmental field has done so poorly incorporating these groups in the past, it must begin planning and adjusting for the future now.

Corporations, government agencies, foundations are expected to put up $5 million to fund the Minorities Opportunities Program. Biennial conferences on the topic will be held, and colleges and universities with large minority populations will be encouraged to establish and expand ES programs. Summer internships will provide minority students with practical experience.

WHERE SHOULD YOU WRITE FOR MORE INFORMATION?

The Alliance for Environmental Education
  (Publication: *Network Exchange*)
  10751 Ambassador Drive, Suite 201
  Manassas, Va. 22110

American Society for Testing and Materials
 New Activity Development
 1916 Race Street
 Philadelphia, Pa. 19103-1187

The CEIP Fund, Inc.
 (Publication: *Connections*)
 68 Harrison Avenue, 5th floor
 Boston, Mass. 02111

ERIC Clearinghouse for Science, Mathematics, and Environmental Education
 Ohio State University
 School of Natural Resources
 1200 Chambers Road, 3rd floor
 Columbus, Ohio 43212

Heldref Publication
 (Publications: *Environment, Journal of Environmental Education*)
 4000 Albemarle Street, N.W., Suite 504
 Washington, D.C. 20016

North American Association for Environmental Education
 (Publication: *Environmental Communicator*)
 Brukner Nature Center
 5995 Horseshoe Bend Road
 P.O. Box 400
 Troy, Ohio 45373

CHAPTER 3

THE SCIENCES OF LIVING THINGS

We base much of what we regard as our civilization—including agriculture, forestry, and medicine—directly on our ability to manipulate the characteristics of plants, animals, and microorganisms. Thus, these discoveries have profound implications for our welfare. They teach us to utilize the productive capacity of the global ecosystem on a sustainable basis.—*Opportunities in Biology*[1]

PROFESSIONS COVERED

Ecology, Biology, Environmental Chemistry

A survey of the biological sciences was issued by the national Research Council in 1970. When, almost twenty years later, a second survey was conducted to update the first, it showed almost breathtaking advances in the field. "[N]o single individual can hope to grasp all of the new activities and opportunities," wrote Dr. Peter H. Raven, director of the Missouri Botanical Garden, St. Louis, and chair of the committee that wrote the current report. It represents consensus of a

---

[1]*Opportunities in Biology,* © 1989 by the National Academy of Sciences, National Academy Press, Washington, D.C.

27

twenty-member committee, which worked for three years and was assisted by more than one hundred other reviewers and contributors. The resulting 448-page book, *Opportunities in Biology,* states:

> During the past two decades, biological research has been transformed from a collection of single-discipline endeavors to an interactive science in which traditional disciplines are being bridged. . . . To encourage the development of new, improved techniques and instrumentation for biology, the barriers separating biology, chemistry, physics, and engineering must be breached by a new generation of well-trained scientists and engineers.

Examples of such techniques are those involving the uses of recombinant DNA, monoclonal antibodies, and microchemical instrumentation.

"The methods necessary for a complete understanding of living systems at the molecular level now seem to be at hand," the panel prophesizes. The areas covered include genes and cells, the nervous system and behavior, the immune system and infectious diseases, and evolution and diversity.

Especially pertinent to environmental education and careers are the conclusions on ecology and ecosystems; medicine, the biochemical process industry, and animal agriculture; and plant biology and agriculture, particularly the findings on training.

ECOLOGY

A group of living components in a natural neighborhood constitutes an ecological system, an *ecosystem,* such as a forest, a lake or an estuary. Larger ecosystems—which occur in a similar climate and have similar vegetation—are called *biomes;* examples are the arctic tundra, prairie grassland, or desert. The *biosphere* is comprised of the earth, with its surrounding envelope of life-sustaining air and water, plus all its living things. All of these are elements of the *environment,* including as well people and social, political, and economic systems. *Ecology* is the discipline that is concerned with all such features and their connections.

"What is ecology?" the Ecological Society of America provides this definition:

> Ecology is the study of interactions among all forms of life, and between organisms and their environments. Ecology is distinguished from other biological sciences by its emphasis on interactions, and from other environmental sciences by its focus on systems inclusive of life.

What Do Ecologists Do?

The ESA further says:

> Ecologists may focus on the natural history of a species of fish or insect, use the data to develop a mathematical theory of patterns of species distribution or may seek to understand the relationship between species diversity and magnitude of pollutants in rivers and lakes. Whatever the focus of study, ecologists seek to understand the basic processes which have formed and maintained these systems and have created their special character.

The majority of ecologists, being on university faculties, teach and conduct research. Most colleges and universities offer courses in ecology. Most universities offer some graduate studies. In the liberal arts colleges offering only undergraduate instruction, teaching is the primary function, research secondary. Many community college and high school teachers also give courses in ecology, especially introductory or fundamentals overviews. Such college and secondary school teachers may participate in ecological research projects on their summer vacations, or they may be working toward graduate degrees during vacation periods or sabbaticals. In these respects, they do not differ from faculty members of major universities.

The third major function, often an adjunct to teaching and research, is administration. An administrator is responsible for keeping books and records which are audited as required by laws and regulations.

Ecologists frequently work in teams; their activities depend on cooperation with and support from others; and the team's results depend greatly on the integrity of each ecologist's contribution.

What Education Would You Need to Become an Ecologist?

The Ecological Society of America, in its careers folder, stresses the importance of early preparation in high school. Take a well-rounded program including biology, mathematics, physics, geology, chemistry, social sciences, and humanities. In college, you might major in the biological sciences, taking courses in morphology, physiology, and genetics, as well as ecology. Inorganic and organic chemistry are essential, and biochemistry and physical chemistry may be important for certain areas of ecology. If you aspire to a research career—and many ecologists do—you should take as much physics and mathematics as possible, including calculus, linear algebra, probability theory, statistics, computer science, and economics. French and German are recommended as the languages of choice, with Russian and Chinese growing in popularity.

In your high school or college years, you should be able to find summer jobs related to ecology, and thereby judge whether you have sufficient interest and aptitude to specialize in this field. Specialization can begin during undergraduate years, with a major in biology, botany, or zoology, with special preparation in general ecology. But a B.S. degree is not sufficient; you should expect to go on for a master's and eventually a doctor's degree. Most professional ecologists hold the Ph.D.

Professional certification is granted by the Ecological Society of America to those who qualify at each of three levels, requiring a successively higher educational degree or depth of experience. The levels are called associate ecologist, ecologist, and senior ecologist.

Where Would You Work as an Ecologist?

Teacher, researcher, or administrator—the ecologist most often fills all three roles simultaneously. Some do research exclusively, as employees of the federal or state government, frequently at an agricultural experiment station of a land grant college. Still others work for private companies in forestry, paper products, or large agricultural operations. Moreover, ecologists study the impacts of energy developments on the environment. Oil and natural gas producers have ecologists on their exploration teams, along with geologists and other earth scientists. Such teams are studying the outer continental shelf, coastal zone, estuaries, and even desert areas to establish baseline conditions before new facilities disrupt the ecology, to monitor the environment while new facilities are being built, and to assure that problems do not arise after these facilities are in operation. Any industry or utility that is planning to build, for example, a power plant in a fragile environment needs to employ an ecologist for such studies.

Most basic research in ecology is sponsored by the National Science Foundation through grants to universities. Other government agencies— primarily the Departments of Agriculture, Interior, and Defense; the Environmental Protection Agency; and the National Oceanic and Atmospheric Administration—are major employing agencies. The United Nations Environment Program, various specialized U.N. agencies, and private philanthropic foundations employ ecologists in international programs.

A job search is time-dependent; ads in Sunday's newspaper frequently are filled by close of business Monday. In many ads appear deadlines for applying. Therefore, examples given for openings cannot be used by a job-seeker; they are, nevertheless, instructive as to the trends which a future applicant should study.

Jobs in ecology, particularly for beginners, are seldom advertised in the general media. Such ads are to be found in specialized newsletters (see lists at the end of this chapter); and jobs at the senior levels are advertised in technical journals read by professionals.

Recent ads in *Science* magazine and other journals list openings for ecologists on various bases: temporary, one-year, permanent; in various parts of the country; with public and private organizations; teaching; research only; outdoors field work; and on land or sea.

In journals and newsletters, one finds openings for a plankton ecologist in Florida, a wetlands ecologist in Illinois; a consultant in New York; and fifty or sixty other openings for which an ecologist might be qualified.

One of the largest advertisers, at this time, is EG&G Measurements, a company supporting Department of Energy environmental programs at Elk Hills Petroleum Reserve, Bakersfield, California, and Nevada

Test Site, Las Vegas, Nevada. It has been soliciting ecologists with B.S., M.S., and Ph.D. degrees to apply for openings created by staff expansion. Specialties included plant and animal ecology, soil science, reclamation habitat impact monitoring, and mitigation. A pre-employment physical which includes drug screening is generally required for such government-contract work.

What Do Ecologists Earn?

Ecology is a small field, the smallest component of the biological sciences. More than half, perhaps a majority, of all ecologists work directly for the federal government. They got their jobs through competitive examination, which means an evaluation of their records compared to other applicants applying for similar jobs at the same time in the same geographical area.

With a bachelor's degree, one would usually begin in the government at the General Schedule grade five (GS-5), with a beginning annual salary in 1991 of $16,875. An entrant with the master's would probably start at grade 7, which pays $20,902 a year. Academic standing and research accomplishments—as well as recommendations of professors, employers, or supervisors—could qualify one for a single grade advance, amounting to perhaps two thousand dollars more. Within each grade there are ten levels paying progressively higher salaries for satisfactory performance. The latest annual increase for federal civilian employees, recommended by the President and approved by Congress, was 3.5 percent, which is about average over recent years. One can assume that federal and nonfederal salaries will indefinitely continue to rise, influenced by economic conditions, at the 2 to 4 percent rate.

According to the College Placement Council, beginning salary offers in private industry in 1988 (the latest year for which figures are available) averaged $20,400 a year for someone with a bachelor's degree in biological science. One can assume that industry salary levels also will continue to rise, in good times or bad, and slightly ahead of comparable government paychecks.

What Is the Job Future for Ecologists?

The Bureau of Labor Statistics (BLS) lumps ecology into the biological sciences; therefore, BLS provides no separate report on employment, or employment prospects, for ecologists alone. As ecology is a component of the biological sciences, it grows and thrives as its larger cousin, biology, grows and thrives.

The *Opportunities* report often cited here foresees "shortages of trained personnel in biology . . . at the bachelor's and master's levels." If the biological sciences community succeeds in building on that report, in mobilizing congressional and public support for the enhancement of biological research, that in turn will create jobs for ecologists as well as other biological scientists. (See "What Is the Job Future for Biologists?" later in this chapter.)

BIOLOGY

The biologist's first commitment is to the traditions of science; the second is to the particular profession of *biology;* and the third to the subdivision of biology in which one practices. Those are the priorities suggested by the American Institute of Biological Sciences (AIBS), which defines its field:

> Biology, the most intriguing and pervasive of sciences, is the study of life and living things. It is actually a multi-science composed of many disciplines unified by the fact that all living things—plants, animals, and microorganisms—follow the same fundamental laws of heredity, reproduction, growth, development, self-maintenance and response.

What Do Biologists Do?

Most scientists probably find their particular disciplines "the most intriguing and pervasive of all sciences" (or they would have chosen some other discipline). Nevertheless, the thrust of the definition is factual. Most scientists are intellectually curious and honest. They enjoy posing hypotheses and testing them against observations. When satisfied with the validity of resulting data, they are eager to publish, to share the information with their peers in a scientific journal, so that others may replicate the experiments, validate (or nullify) the results, and contribute substantiating evidence and additional data. By such shared endeavors is all science advanced.

Ecology is called a *biological science* "distinguished by its emphasis on interactions. . . . and its focus on systems inclusive of life." Other specialists in the biological sciences (*biosciences,* for short) might or might not consider themselves *environmental scientists,* although often the consequences of their work have notable environmental applications and implications. The biologist who studies plants is a *botanist;* and the one who studies animals a *zoologist.* Another, who studies form and structure, including development, is a *developmental biologist.* Yet another who studies the function of whole organisms and their components is a *physiologist.* The one concerned with the heredity mechanisms which control both structure and function is a *geneticist.* He or she who studies the evolution and classification of plants and animals is a *systematist* or *taxonomist.*

What Education Would You Need to Become a Biologist?

To become a biologist you should have as much high school science and mathematics as possible, preferably four years of each. You should have a bachelor's degree. Virtually every college and university provides training in biology to the B.S. or B.A. level. An environmental studies curriculum, such as described in Chapter 2, should include much biology. Professional jobs in biological research are difficult for the bachelor's graduate to find. You can maximize your employability, however, by taking courses in English, chemistry, physics, and mathematics, as well as statistics and computer sciences.

When you are ready and able to begin postgraduate studies, by all means do so. Graduate school need not follow immediately upon receipt of the bachelor's degree. Many students are neither psychologically ready nor financially able to go on to graduate school right after college. Take the best available job, even though it may be beneath the level for which you are qualified. It will afford useful experience, provide income to meet later graduate school expenses, and give you a "breather," a change of pace, even a chance to move to a new city or a new part of the country.

Alternate periods of work and study are often the student's best course. Such a plan lets you put theory into practice, provides practical experience essential to advancement, helps make choices on career goals and objectives, and allows perspective on personal as well as professional decisions. Those are the reasons that cooperative education, for example, has been so successful at many schools of engineering, and why many colleges and universities require internships of all undergraduates.

Many employers, public and private, provide such incentives to graduate study as time off with pay, tuition and fees, and sometimes living and other expenses. At least, an employer satisfied with an employee's work may hold open the job while he or she is away for further learning.

Membership in professional societies is optional, and there are no licenses or registrations required for the biologist. As in other sciences, one's peers exert pressure to publish research findings and to participate in professional activities. Even so, this pressure would be felt largely by the biologist on the college or university faculty, not on the one in industry or government.

Where Would You Work as a Biologist?

The largest fraction of biologists is engaged in teaching and research at colleges and universities. The next largest works in private industry, especially in pharmaceuticals, chemicals, and food processing. The third largest segment is employed in state and local government agencies and in the Departments of Agriculture and the Interior, the National Institutes of Health, and the armed services. Finally, a few thousand work for nonprofit research organizations.

Biologists are distributed fairly evenly throughout the United States and Canada because higher education and industry are so widely dispersed. But employment is concentrated in metropolitan centers or on college campuses.

With only a bachelor's degree, you would have limited possibilities for advancement in research and development or other professional tracks. New graduates at this level often get testing and inspecting jobs or become technical sales and service representatives. With courses in education, you might become a secondary school biology teacher. A master's degree is essential for a senior position in industry or a college faculty appointment.

What Do Biologists Earn?

As shown earlier for ecologists, biological scientists generally, when they have only a bachelor's degree, would begin in the federal government at the GS-5 level. This carries a beginning annual salary of $16,875.

According to the College Placement Council, beginning salary offers in private industry in 1988 averaged $20,000 a year for bachelor's degree recipients in biological science.

Want to earn almost twice that amount, in Alaska, with "strenuous working conditions, but supportive company"? The company advertising is a consulting firm, which offers a training class every month, $2,450 to $3,000 per month, and year-round opportunities. Duties would be observing, collecting, sorting, and recording sample catches on board commercial fishing boats. Qualifications include a B.S. in biology "and a flexible attitude"—no experience required.

The Nature Conservancy, a major conservation group, often seeks conservation workers at various locations—Sioux Falls, South Dakota; Honolulu, Hawaii; Charlottesville, Virginia; and others. Some, but not many, of these openings are for beginners.

A new field for the sales-and-promotion minded individual is that of "environmental activist," a common euphemism for fundraiser or solicitor. Greenpeace, Clean Water Action Project, and Public Citizen's Critical Mass Energy Project are among the national groups that raise significant portions of their budgets by door-to-door or telephone solicitation. Jobs are to be found through classified ads in many metropolitan newspapers. Students may do this during summer vacations and may join teams that travel from city to city for special campaigns. Offerings start at about $16,000 and seldom go above $24,000. Remuneration is generally on commission, that is, a percentage of funds raised.

Many universities frequently offer graduate or teaching fellowships at low wages but with such incentives as tuition waivers.

What Is the Job Future for Biologists?

The BLS expects employment of biological scientists to increase faster than the average for all occupations through the year 2000. Almost half of the total of more than 100,000 professional biologists (including ecologists) teach at the college level, and this segment is not expected to increase very much. The BLS breaks out the 57,000 nonacademics and expects this segment to grow at the faster-than-average rate of 26 percent, or 15,000 more individuals to be employed by the year 2000.

Most growth is expected to be in private industry (unless the Congress is prodded by the biological-science community to implement the recommendations of *Opportunities in Biology,* as discussed below).

That optimistic forecast is supported by recent trends. Consider the advertisements cited in the section above. One thing such advertising indicates is that a biological sciences background is so broad it qualifies a graduate for a significant number of openings, at almost any time.

"More biological scientists will be needed to determine the environmental impacts of industry and government actions and to correct past environmental problems," states the *Occupational Outlook Handbook,* the biennial compilation by the Bureau of Labor Statistics. "Many persons with bachelor's degrees in biological science find jobs as science or engineering technicians or health technologists, or—with teacher accreditation—as high school science teachers."

(Without documentation, the handbook finds, "Biological scientists are less likely to lose their jobs during recessions than those in many other occupations since most are employed on long-term research projects or in agricultural research, activities which are not much affected by economic fluctuations.")

On a more long-range basis, *Opportunities in Biology* predicts a bright future for the field. One area is *biotechnology,* defined by the National Science Foundation and the Office of Technology Assessment as a technique that uses living organisms or parts of organisms to make or modify products, to improve plants or animals, or to develop micro-organisms for specific uses. The *Opportunities* panel wrote:

> Shortages of trained technical personnel in biology are now occurring at the bachelor's and master's levels. Attempts should be made to enhance university training programs at these levels, especially in bio-technology-related areas (biochemistry, cell biology, microbiology, im-munology, molecular genetics, and bioprocess engineering). Shortages of Ph.D.s in biotechnology-related areas are anticipated (as well) in the late 1990s. Also needed will be instrumentation technicians.

The five main areas of research and development in biotechnology are health care, plant agriculture, chemicals and food additives, animal agriculture, and energy and the environment.

An exciting early application of biotechnology is in biomedicine. The human gene that codes for the production of insulin has been inserted into bacteria, causing the bacteria to produce human insulin. This insulin, used to treat diabetes, is much purer than insulin from animals, the only previous source. Other substances not previously available in large quantities are starting to be produced by biotechnological means; a number are on the brink of approval for treating cancer and other diseases.

Of special interest to environmentalists is another new area, *conservation biology,* whose responsibility is understanding, and preventing the crises in, habitat degradation and species extinction. *Opportunities* states:

> Over the next several decades, conservation biology will focus in-creasing attention on the restoration of degraded or destroyed ecosys-tems. . . . One of the highest priorities for conservation biology, for example, is reforestation in tropical countries with serious deforestation problems. It is difficult to protect, let alone to justify, nature reserves in third-world tropical countries when people [there] have neither timber nor firewood.

Conservation biologists also are attempting to slow the rate of species extinction in rain forest and other environments through improved land management, the formation of seed banks, and the search for alternative fuels.

"There has never been a time when any field of science could be more promising for human welfare and for basic understanding than biology is at present," Dr. Peter Raven summed up in releasing the *Opportunities* report.

Again and again, the report returns to its central theme: That bright future will be realized only if the nation—particularly through the government—comes soon to recognize the urgency of the need and commits more funds for advanced education, facilities, and basic research.

ENVIRONMENTAL CHEMISTRY

Chemistry is the science of the composition, structure, properties, and reactions of matter, including its atomic and molecular systems. Chemistry often is considered an environmental science in its own right, and the American Chemical Society publishes the journal *ES&T: Environmental Science & Technology*. An environmental emphasis may enter into any of the major subfields of chemistry, as well.

What Do Environmental Chemists Do?

The *analytical chemist* determines the structure, composition, and nature of substances and develops new techniques. Originally, the *organic chemist* studied the chemistry of living things, but this area has been broadened to include all carbon compounds. When combined with other elements, carbon forms an incredible variety of substances. Many modern commercial products, including plastics and other synthetics, have resulted from work in organic chemistry. The *inorganic chemist* studies compounds other than carbon and may develop, for example, materials for use in solid state electronic components. The *physical chemist* studies energy transformations to find new and better energy sources. The *toxicologist* conducts tests on animals to determine the effects of drugs, gases, poisons, pesticides, radiation, and other substances on the health of the organism. The *biochemist* or *biophysicist* studies the chemical and physical behavior of living things. Since life is based on complex chemical combinations and reactions, the work of the biochemist is vital for an understanding of the basic functions of living things such as reproduction and growth. The biochemist also may investigate the effects of substances such as food, hormones, or drugs on various organisms.

The *chemical engineer* is involved in many phases of research on chemicals and byproducts and their production and may be involved in pollution control and environmental protection.

What Education Would You Need to Become an Environmental Chemist?

Nearly every college and university offers a basic degree in chemistry. Only selected engineering colleges offer a chemical engineering degree. More than 350 institutions offer graduate degrees in chemistry. Graduate students generally are required to have a bachelor's degree in chemistry, biology, or biochemistry. Many graduate schools emphasize some specialties of chemistry over others because of the type of research being done at those institutions. If you lean toward a certain type of environmental career, you should pick your graduate school with that leaning in mind. Graduate training requires actual research in addition to advanced science courses. For the doctoral degree, you specialize in one field of chemistry by doing intensive research and by writing a dissertation.

Where Would You Work as an Environmental Chemist?

Of the eighty-thousand chemists in the United States, about 60 percent work for manufacturing firms; more than three-fifths of these are in the chemical manufacturing industry or in food processing. Chemists also work for state and local governments, primarily in health and agriculture, and for federal agencies, chiefly the Departments of Defense, Health and Human Services, and Agriculture. About nineteen-thousand chemists are on the faculties of colleges and universities.

Jobs are distributed throughout the United States and Canada, especially in metropolitan areas, on college campuses, and at agricultural and other research stations.

There are about fifty-thousand chemical engineers as well, mostly in the chemical and petroleum refining industries. Opportunities to travel and live overseas abound for them, especially in the oil industry in oil-producing regions such as the Persian Gulf.

How many of the total employment would be defined as environmental chemists or chemical engineers is problematical. Although the American Chemical Society recognizes the modifier *environmental*—it publishes the monthly journal *ES&T: Environmental Science & Technology*—the Bureau of Labor Statistics has no such category, so any analysis would be guesswork, and meaningless.

We have what is called ''anecdotal evidence,'' as in the classified ads appearing in that journal and in newspapers and newsletters.

What Do Environmental Chemists Earn?

According to the College Placement Council, chemists with a bachelor's degree were offered starting salaries averaging $26,000 a year in 1988; those with a master's degree, $31,600; and those with a Ph.D., $41,300.

Federal salaries pale by comparison. With a bachelor's degree, one would usually begin in the government at the GS-5 level, with a beginning annual salary in 1991 of $16,875. An entrant with the master's would probably start at grade 7, which pays $20,902 a year. (For other comments applicable to chemists and chemical engineers, see ''What Do Ecologists Earn?'' and ''What Do Biologists Earn?'' earlier in this chapter.)

In a survey by the American Chemical Society, median salaries of their experienced members with a bachelor's degree were $35,600 a year in 1988; with a master's, $41,000; and with a Ph.D., $50,000.

Chemists and chemical engineers frequently advance to management positions. Here, the salary levels are significantly higher than—sometimes more than twice as high as—any cited above. Major chemical-industry corporations employ environmental department directors, often at the vice-presidential level, and at very high salaries commensurate with their enormous responsibilities.

Increasingly, many large chemical companies are offering a dual-track career plan. One track is for management and marketing positions; this is the traditional career ladder to higher-paying positions. What is new is the so-called technical ladder. Qualified persons can choose to remain working at the laboratory bench, doing research, publishing, competing only with one's peers for promotions, getting promoted regularly to higher salaries, enjoying opportunities to travel, and participating as an officer in a national or international scientific society.

What Is the Job Future for Environmental Chemists?

According to the *Occupational Outlook Handbook:*

> Chemists are expected to have very good employment opportunities through the year 2000. . . . Employment is expected to grow because of expanded research and development—for new products and more efficient production process, and because more will be needed in environmental protection efforts. Also, the chemical industry, which faced many problems in the early 1980s, is now much healthier. Areas relating to pharmaceuticals, biotechnology, and environmental protection should provide especially good opportunities.

The BLS makes a further, pertinent point about a large industry such as chemicals: Even when it is growing far more slowly than a small field such as ecology, the smaller percentage of openings created amounts to a large total number.

A recent article in *Chemecology,* a Chemical Manufacturers Association publication, asks, "What can you do with a chemistry degree?" It quotes Professor T.C. Ichniowski, of Illinois State University, who says that an undergraduate or advanced degree in chemistry "can be a ticket to a career in business, sales, journalism, or law." He mentions having read that a Chicago patent law firm was seeking bachelor-level chemists to provide their lawyers with guidance in biotechnology and bioengineering. And he especially recommends that chemists consider teaching in elementary and secondary schools, if they are willing to take teachers' salaries.

WHERE SHOULD YOU WRITE FOR MORE INFORMATION?

American Association for the Advancement of Science
   (Publication: *Science*)
   1333 H Street, N.W.
   Washington, D.C. 20005

American Chemical Society
   (Publication: *ES&T: Environmental Science & Technology*)
   1155 16th Street, N.W.
   Washington, D.C. 20036

American Institute of Biological Sciences
   (Publication: *Bioscience*)
   Office of Career Service
   730 11th Street, N.W.
   Washington, D.C. 20001-4585

American Institute of Chemical Engineers
   (Publication: *Chemical Engineering*)
   345 East 47th Street
   New York, N.Y. 10017

American Society for Microbiology
   Board of Education and Training
   1325 Massachusetts Avenue, N.W.
   Washington, D.C. 20005

American Society of Zoologists
   Box 2739
   California Lutheran College
   Thousand Oaks, Calif. 91320

Botanical Society of America
   c/o Dr. Gregory Anderson, Secretary
   Department of Ecology, U-43
   75 North Eagleville Road
   Storrs, Conn. 0629969-3043

Chemical Manufacturers Association
(Publication: *Chemecology*)
2501 M Street, N.W.
Washington, D.C. 20037

Ecological Society of America
Public Affairs Office
9650 Rockville Pike, Suite 2503
Bethesda, Md. 20814

National Association of Biology Teachers
11250 Roger Bacon Drive, No. 19
Reston, Va. 22090

Society for Human Ecology
1401 Marie Mount Hall
University of Maryland
College Park, Md. 20742

SUBSCRIPTION NEWSLETTERS LISTING CURRENT OPENINGS IN ALL ENVIRONMENTAL FIELDS

Environmental Job Opportunities
Institute for Environmental Studies
University of Wisconsin-Madison
550 North Park Street, 15 Science Hall
Madison, Wisc. 53706

Environmental Opportunities
P.O. Box 4957
Arcata, Calif. 95521

The Job Seeker
Route 2, Box 16
Warrens, Wisc. 54666

GUIDES TO A JOB SEARCH

(Available at libraries)

Conservation Directory, published annually by National Wildlife Federation, 1412 16th Street, N.W., Washington, D.C. 20036.

Occupational Outlook Handbook, published biennially by Bureau of Labor Statistics, U.S. Department of Labor, and *Occupational Outlook Quarterly,* both for sale from Superintendent of Documents, U.S. Government Printing Office, Washington, D.C. 20402-9325.

CHAPTER 4

ENVIRONMENTAL PROTECTION AND PUBLIC HEALTH

People have only to conserve plant and animal life, and the resources of the earth, to share in nature's bounty and beauty. But they can also suffer because of this close relationship with nature: Many diseases pass from animals, insects, and soil to humans. The beautiful blue heron, like the golden-haired child with diphtheria, can be the source of disease.— *Tracking Diseases from Nature to Man* (Centers for Disease Control)

PROFESSIONS COVERED

Environmental Engineering, Environmental Health Sciences, Environmental Medicine (including Environmental Nursing and Public Health Veterinary Medicine), Environmental Sanitation, Health Physics, Industrial Hygiene

In August 1970 the newly established Council on Environmental Quality (CEQ), in its first report on the state of the nation's environment, was guardedly optimistic about what lay ahead in environmental protection and public health. By 1989, it was possible for the CEQ to devote hundreds of pages of its twentieth report[1] to detailing such accomplishments as these:

---

[1]Council on Environmental Quality, *Environmental Quality: Twentieth Annual Report of the Council on Environmental Quality,* 494 pp., Washington, D.C.: Superintendent of Documents, U.S. Government Printing Office, 1989.

In the two decades that followed the singular events of 1970, the nation's growing concern for the environment manifested itself in a dozen major—and several dozen minor—federal environmental laws. By 1989 the federal government had acquired regulatory responsibilities addressing air quality, water quality, drinking water, solid wastes, hazardous wastes, medical wastes, pesticides, toxic substances, endangered species, occupational safety and health, coastal zones, ocean pollution, and the upper atmosphere, among others.

A seventy-one-page chapter on environmental enforcement is devoted to how a dozen federal agencies are actively enforcing twenty-one environmental laws. They include Superfund, which brought over $800 million in consent decrees and reimbursements in one recent year alone!

ENVIRONMENTAL PROTECTION AND
PUBLIC HEALTH: CURRENT STIRRINGS

In a new report from the Environmental Protection Agency's (EPA's) science advisory board, the emphasis is on reducing risks.[2] It says, "Since this country already has taken the most obvious actions to address the most obvious environmental problems, EPA needs to set priorities for future actions so the Agency takes advantage of the best opportunities for reducing the most serious remaining risks"—both ecological and human health risks. Tools suggested include data and analytical methodologies, strategic planning, economic analyses, market incentives, pollution prevention, and improved public understanding. The panel further observed:

> The nation is facing a shortage of environmental scientists and engineers needed to cope with environmental problems today and in the future. It is strongly recommended that EPA provide technical and financial assistance to universities to help them incorporate environmen-

---

[2]Science Advisory Board: Relative Risk Reduction Strategies Committee, *Reducing Risk: Setting Priorities and Strategies for Environmental Protection* (Washington, D.C.: U.S. Environmental Protection Agency, 1990).

tal subject matter into their curricula and to train the next generation of environmental scientists and engineers.

As Dr. Jay D. Hair notes in his Foreword to this book, a synergism exists between the public and private sectors. Conservationists and corporate executives are sitting down in many forums to address environmental concerns of mutual and national interest. Corporate advertising is frequently devoted to these concerns.

Industry has three economic incentives to prevent the generation of wastes. First, pollution control, cleanup, and liability costs are rising rapidly, as the Superfund results mentioned above and again below show. Second, costs of resource inputs—energy and raw materials—are increasing as well, further encouraging their efficient use.

Finally, public pressure on companies to decrease pollution has mounted, magnified by new requirements under section 313 of the Superfund Amendments that makes firms report annual releases of toxic chemicals. This law, the Emergency Planning and Community Right-to-Know Act, produced in 1987 more than 75,000 reports of violations of pollution-control regulations; all of this information was immediately disclosed to the public. (Industries and communities have the added incentive of publicity.)

Major corporations are taking expensive steps to comply with environmental regulations. Sometimes belatedly, these corporations are beginning to turn a profit in recycling and resource recovery. Take three examples from the chemical conglomerate Du Pont, which is spending about $1 billion a year on environmental control:

One of its product lines everybody is familiar with is plastic bottles. Du Pont makes two types of common plastics—polyethylene terepthalate (PET) and high-density polyethylene (HDPE)—for, respectively, large soft-drink bottles and ordinary soft-drink and plastic milk bottles. After use, the empties are hard to get rid of, so Du Pont operates plants in which plastic bottles are ground up and the two types of plastic separated. The resulting plastic flakes are sent to other company plants to be made into other products. In a second example, Du Pont services one thousand accounts in treating their hazardous wastes as well as its own. The company also will buy back common refrigerants like chlorofluoro-carbon (CFC) for reprocessing by distillation. All of this is new with the world's largest chemical company, whose chairman and chief executive since 1989, Edgar S. Woolard, Jr., calls himself "the company's chief environmentalist."

In poll after poll, a majority of Americans support rigorous environment control. For instance, a 1990 survey by The Roper Organization, sponsored by S.C. Johnson and Son, Inc., found 61 percent of Americans pin the blame for environmental degradation on industry. Asked about current environmental laws and regulations, 69 percent felt they were inadequate, 17 percent were comfortable with them, and only 4 percent said government has gone too far.

"HEALTHY PEOPLE 2000"

Environmental protection and public health is a major component of a massive report entitled *Healthy People 2000* and issued by the Department of Health and Human Services in 1990.[3] By the year 2000—hence the date in the title—the American people should achieve 298 specific health objectives. The report says:

> The most difficult challenges for environmental health today come not from what *is known* about the harmful effects of microbial agents; rather they come from what *is not known* about the toxic and ecologic effects of the use of fossil fuels and synthetic chemicals in modern society. Population growth, urbanization, new energy sources, advanced technology, industrialization, and modern agricultural methods have enabled unprecedented progress. At the same time, they have created hazards to human health that are dramatically different from hazards in the past. Synthetic chemicals, new sources of toxic substances, and naturally occurring radiation are distributed throughout the environment. The potential risks from many of these agents were initially either unrecognized, underestimated, or accepted as inevitable and minor in comparison to the benefits of modernization and economic growth. . . .

---

[3]Department of Health and Human Services, *Healthy People 2000: National Health Promotion and Disease Prevention Objectives,* 671 pp., Washington, D.C.: Superintendent of Documents, U.S. Government Printing Office, 1990.

There are significant gaps in our knowledge about exposures to environmental agents in both indoor and outdoor air, in ground and surface water, in the atmosphere, in soils and wetlands, and in plants and animals, including sources of human food. Sophisticated methods to identify very small quantities of substances must be adapted to create cost-effective and cost-efficient methods for making accurate measures of environmental contamination over significant periods of time.

The specific objectives in environmental health are aimed at targets to be reached by the year 2000, measured from baselines between 1987 and 1991. They include reducing morbidity in asthma, mental retardation among school-aged children, outbreaks of waterborne disease, the prevalence of high blood lead levels in small children, and human exposure to air pollutants and toxic agents.

Water pollution and solid waste-related water, air, and soil contamination also would be reduced. Drinking water supplies would be improved. Homes would be tested for lead-based paint contamination and radon concentrations. Programs for recyclable materials and household hazardous waste would be extended to counties now lacking them.

PROFESSIONALISM

There are several marks that are especially important in environmental health whereby one becomes, and is identified as, a *professional.* The most common is *membership in a professional association,* a privilege usually accorded anyone who graduates from an accredited college or university with a degree in the discipline. The principal professional organizations listed at the end of this and other chapters are examples. These associations provide services such as professional education and information to their members, career information to students, and general information and services to the public. They represent the profession in dealing with other professional organizations, with regulatory and licensing bodies, and in lobbying in Washington and state capitals.

Certification is the process by which a nongovernmental agency or association (such as a professional organization just mentioned) grants recognition to an individual who has met certain predetermined qualifications.

Registration is the process by which qualified individuals are listed on an official roster maintained by a governmental or nongovernmental agency. Within some professions there are specialty boards or registries established by the professions themselves. These boards identify those members of the profession who meet certain requirements of education, experience and competence, as determined through examination. Such individuals may be accorded the title of "Fellow" or "Diplomate."

Licensure is the process by which an agency of government grants permission to persons meeting predetermined qualifications to engage in a given occupation which directly affects the health and welfare of the public. Sometimes the license permits these persons to use a particular title. More than thirty occupations in the health field are licensed in one or more states. All fifty states and the District of Columbia require licensure of civil engineers, environmental health engineers, and others when they are engaged in engineering work which may affect life, health, or property—and who offer their services to the public on a fee basis. The initials P.E. after a person's name stand for Professional Engineer, a mark of professional distinction. All states, territories, and the District of Columbia also require licensure for physicians (Medical Doctor, M.D., and Doctor of Osteopathy, D.O.).

ENVIRONMENTAL ENGINEERING

As an *environmental engineer,* you would command the specialized engineering knowledge essential to solve environmental problems which are engineering in nature. Because so many environmental problems are *interdisciplinary/integrated/involved,* increasingly the engineer is *the* key member of the management team.

Engineering is defined as the means by which the properties of matter and the sources of energy in nature are applied to practical purposes. The first engineers in America held a combination of civil and military roles. For example, George Washington is regarded as the father of the engineering profession as well as the father of his country. Civil engineers laid out plans for cities and designed and supervised the construction of roads, harbors, tunnels, and bridges. Then, as now, civil engineers with additional specialized training in sanitation and called *sanitary engineers* were responsible for designing and building safe public water supplies and wastewater treatment facilities and controlling flying/crawling vectors of disease such as flies and mosquitoes. By controlling the mosquitoes which carry malaria and yellow fever, the sanitary engineer made possible the building of the Panama Canal where the French had failed because of those diseases' toll. The sanitary engineer designed the sanitation facilities which have made our cities the world's healthiest urban environments.

While sanitation is still a part of the job, this practice of engineering today is much broader. To reflect the broader responsibilities, this practitioner more likely goes by the title of *environmental engineer*. The practice is a subset of civil engineering.

What Do Environmental Engineers Do?

In its recruiting brochure "Is Civil Engineering for You?" the American Society of Civil Engineers (ASCE) describes the duties:

> As a civil engineer, you plan, design, and supervise the construction of facilities essential to modern life in both the public and private sectors—facilities that vary widely in nature, size and scope: space satellites and launching facilities, off-shore structures, bridges, buildings, tunnels, highways, transit systems, dams, airports, irrigation projects, treatment and distribution facilities for [drinking] water and collection and treatment facilities for wastewater.

ASCE emphasizes that civil engineers are among the leading users of today's sophisticated high technology. The latest concepts in computer-aided design (CAD) are employed during design, construction, project scheduling, and cost control phases of any complicated construction project.

Contributions to community development and environmental improvement also are emphasized by ASCE:

Civil engineers are problem solvers, meeting the challenges of pollution, the deteriorating infrastructure, traffic congestion, energy needs, floods, earthquakes, urban redevelopment, and community planning. You will be a doer. You will be responsible for improving the quality of life in these areas and many more. Service to the community, its development and improvement, is basically what civil engineering is all about.

The energy industry is a major employer of environmental engineers. They assess the potential environmental impact of a new power plant, oil refinery, offshore oil rig, electrical transmission line, or oil or gas pipeline, before it is built; monitor it while it is being built; and assure that it operates correctly and safely. They use an array of monitoring instruments and techniques to detect trouble before it arises and, if possible, to avert it.

The environmental engineer is responsible, too, for providing engineering leadership or support to programs of hazardous wastes control, noise abatement, public safety, resource conservation, toxic substances control, regional planning and land use, and literally hundreds of others. Even in the inner cities, environmental engineers are adding to their traditional roles of sanitation and insect and rat control such new initiatives as programs to prevent traffic accidents, mitigate lead poisoning from paint and from auto emissions, rehabilitate housing, and provide community amenities. New technology such as computers and computer simulation models make the work of environmental engineers more efficient when used to model and manage systems such as for drinking water and wastewater.

What Education Would You Need
to Become an Environmental Engineer?

More than two hundred institutions in the United States offer accredited programs in civil engineering, under which environmental engineering usually falls. Most programs require four years of study for the bachelor's degree. A typical four-year curriculum consists of approximately one year of mathematics and basic sciences; one year of engineering science and analysis; one year of engineering theory and design;

and one year that includes social sciences, humanities, communications, ethics, and professionalism, along with electives which complement the overall cultural education of the individual.

Although many still begin their civil engineering careers on the basis of a bachelor's degree, more than one-third of all such graduates today go on to earn a master's degree. Some universities offer a five-year program leading to a bachelor's after the fourth year and a master's at the end of the fifth. Many liberal arts colleges have arrangements with university engineering schools whereby a student can spend three years at the college and two years at the university and receive a bachelor's degree from each institution. Some engineering colleges have cooperative, "co-op," programs—five- or six-year plans under which the student alternates between schooling and employment.

All fifty states, the District of Columbia, and the U.S. territories have enacted legislation requiring the registration of engineers. The rationale is that registration safeguards life, health, and property and promotes the general welfare. Still, registration is a voluntary process, generally achieved by compliance with educational, experience, and examination requirements.

The examination is given in two parts. ASCE encourages the young engineer to take the first exam as soon after graduation as possible. It provides the Engineer-in-Training (EIT) certificate. This exam, titled Fundamentals of Engineering, takes eight hours. The second part, Principles and Practice of Engineering, also eight hours, is taken approximately four years later. Success in passing this exam qualifies one to use the initials P.E. (for Professional Engineer) after the name.

Engineers in private practice must be registered, depending on their level of responsibility. Most engineers in federal, state, or municipal government need to be registered. Registration of engineers in industry is not required, since many states have an industrial exemption in their statutes. However, recent legal events relating to product liability, and to the qualifications needed to serve in court as expert witnesses, have led many companies to encourage their engineers to become registered. With recent changes in attitude by industry and engineering societies in support of voluntary registration, an increasing number of engineers will find professional registration essential in order to maximize their career development.

Through reciprocity/comity, registration in one jurisdiction generally is recognized in another, without further examination.

Where Would You Work as an Environmental Engineer?

The traditional employers of environmental engineers, according to the Association of Environmental Engineering Professors, have been local governmental units such as city or county health departments, state governments, and federal agencies. New federal laws such as the Toxic Substance Control Act, Resource Conservation and Recovery Act, and the Comprehensive Environmental Response, Compensation, and Liability Act—better known as Superfund—have created job opportunities both in federal agencies and in the private sector. The greatest job growth recently has been in consulting engineering firms and in the environmental engineering departments of industrial firms. They employ environmental engineers for research and studies on contract, to prepare and evaluate environmental impact statements, and to assure compliance of their client companies with the myriad governmental laws and regulations to which they are subject.

Manufacturers from every major sector—aircraft, aluminum, electrical equipment, industrial chemicals, logging and lumber, motor vehicles, nuclear energy, paper, petroleum refining, and textiles, just to name a few—employ environmental engineers. So do companies in coal mining and petroleum and natural gas production, processing, and distribution by pipeline, ship, or truck; transportation—aviation, railroads, and trucking; public utilities—electric power, cable television, telephones, and microwave towers; and real estate and land development companies.

Interested in adventure overseas? The armed services offer some of the more attractive opportunities for environmental engineering practice. Increasingly, consulting engineering and construction firms with contracts with the oil-producing nations of the Middle East advertise for environmental engineers, among others. They are building, in addition to oil and natural gas facilities, whole new cities, industrial complexes, ports, university campuses, highways, and airports—in fact, entire new "developed" nations are springing up on the desert. Consequently they need significant numbers of environmental engineers.

The developing nations of Africa, South America, and the Pacific also are undertaking enormous development projects, funded by international lending agencies such as the World Bank or the Asian Bank. The work actually is done by multinational engineering and construction companies—U.S., British, Dutch, Japanese, or others. One requirement on the firms, enforced through the client governments, is that the contractors adhere to standards similar to those imposed on federal agencies in the United States by the National Environmental Policy Act. This means that the engineering and construction firms doing the actual work of building a hydroelectric system, reforesting millions of acres, or controlling insect pests are required to engage the services of environmental consultants before getting the funding to undertake the project. Then, throughout construction, they must follow the recommendations of these consultants. Environmental engineers often are the key members of these evaluation and approval teams.

What Do Environmental Engineers Earn?

Civil engineering—of which environmental is a sub-specialty—traditionally has been the lowest-paying of the ten branches of engineering. According to the College Placement Council, in 1988 engineering graduates with a bachelor's degree averaged about $29,200 to start in private industry. Civil engineers averaged only $25,596.

Presumably, this lower compensation is connected to the fact that about 40 percent of all civil engineers work for federal, state, and local governments—which are notorious for paying civil servants the lowest possible salaries. This observation is borne out by many ads in newsletters, where the state of Delaware advertised in 1990 for experienced environmental engineers at $29,000 per annum; New York State offered $26,000; and Nevada, $27,000.

On the other hand, ads abound with more generous salary offers. The U.S. Army hires engineers for hazardous waste cleanup in Europe, up to the GS-11 level, starting in 1990 at $30,937. The same state agency in Delaware mentioned above had higher-level engineering jobs open at $33,000 and $38,000. A New York company sought a sales engineer at $40,000. The state of Washington paid up to $50,000 for a chief engineer in its Department of Natural Resources. And many consulting firms list multiple openings without specifying salaries.

What Is the Job Future for Environmental Engineers?

The Bureau of Labor Statistics expects employment of civil engineers to increase between 11 and 19 percent through the year 2000. As total employment for C.E.'s in 1988 was about 186,000, this is a tremendous pool to replace and augment. (Statistics are not available on what proportion of this number is environmental engineers.)

Environmental engineers continue to be in strong demand by industrial and consulting firms, if the evidence derived from recruitment listings and advertising is to be believed.

Federal agencies also advertise. The Environmental Protection Agency has stepped up its advertising because of added responsibilities the Congress has given it in enforcement, along with higher appropriations. The EPA now has the responsibility of enforcing pollution laws governing air, water, hazardous wastes, and toxics and pesticides. Through ten EPA regional offices, its engineering enforcement personnel cooperate with U.S. attorneys and others, often from state and local bodies, to enforce a number of statutes. These laws include the Clean Air Act Amendments of 1990; Clean Water and Safe Drinking Water Acts; Toxic Substance Control Act; Resource Conservation and Recovery Act; and the Comprehensive Environmental Response, Compensation, and Liability Act (Superfund).

After years of debate and controversy, late in 1990 the Congress passed, and President George Bush signed into law, the Clean Air Act of 1990. It seeks in part to achieve the unrealized objectives of the basic clean air law passed in 1970. It is likely to have a major impact on American industry and will cost $25 billion to implement. Consumers will pay higher prices for new cars, gasoline, electricity, dry cleaning, and a host of products containing newly regulated chemicals. The bill, in print, is 748 pages long. (The original law was only forty-one pages!) Following are some of its major provisions:

- The law's largest economic incentives are in a provision on acid rain. This provision sets an overall annual level of emissions of sulfur dioxide from power plants of 8.9 million tons by the year 2000—less than half the present levels. If a utility reduces emissions below the required level, it can sell the difference as a credit to new or expanding power plants. The proposal for credits was developed by a citizen organization, the Environmental Defense Fund.

- The states are required to meet timetables for smog reduction. Businesses such as bakeries, print shops, and dry cleaners must install control technology. Gasoline to be sold in the nine smoggiest cities must be reformulated to meet tighter emission standards.

- Industrial emitters of 189 airborne toxics are required to install "maximum achievable control technology" by the year 2003. If there is a cancer risk, the EPA is to impose even tighter standards.

- Production of CFCs and halons, a similar chemical used in fire extinguishers, is to be halted by the year 2000, the deadline already imposed by an international treaty. Production of less-corrosive CFC substitutes is to be eliminated as early in the next century as possible. A recycling program for CFCs in air conditioning and refrigeration equipment is mandated by 1992.

- Finally, $50 million a year is to be appropriated for benefits for workers displaced as a result of the Clean Air Act. To qualify, employees who have been laid off must enter and remain in retraining at least halfway through the twenty-six weeks of regular unemployment insurance eligibility.

After enactment of the Clean Air Act Amendments of 1990, the Department of Health and Human Services began reappraising its *Healthy People 2000* objectives. One goal developed before 1990 was to increase the total of 121,000 environmental health specialists identified earlier. The Clean Air Act Amendments, alone, will require a majority of any new number of specialists, and probably a much different mix from before.

ENVIRONMENTAL HEALTH SCIENCES

This is the science counterpart to the environmental engineer. Its practitioner may have been educated in the life sciences, the physical sciences, or the social and behavioral sciences and may have one or more degrees in ecology, biology, or chemistry. The graduate school education may be in agronomy, anatomy, animal science, bacteriology, biochemistry, botany, embryology, microbiology, pathology, pharmacology, physiology, zoology—the list could go on and on. The important distinction from the disciplinary scientist is that in the course of such a person's career, a new turn has been taken. It has been a turn toward the new environmentalism—*interdisciplinary/integrated/involved.*

What Do Environmental Health Scientists Do?

As an *environmental health scientist,* you would hold a key position on a team concerned with environmental protection or public health. You would be in command of the specialized knowledge, often scientific, connected with environmental problems. You would be aware of, and sensitive to, the concerns of others. You would assume command of the team when its assignments were largely scientific. Frequently you would: (a) search for, detect, and analyze environmental pollutants; (b) characterize and study the biological effects of pollutants (or of things such as noise which cause stress and are called "stressors"); (c) determine their epidemiological character (meaning the distribution geographically or through populations, as an epidemic disease might spread); and (d) devise criteria and standards for abating the pollutants or otherwise solving the environmental health problems.

Because this is such a broad category, and its practitioners frequently add management degrees to their scientific skills, you will find many environmental health scientists occupying middle-level or top administrative positions in which they run programs and supervise others.

What Education Would You Need
to Become an Environmental Health Scientist?

A bachelor's degree in biology, chemistry, or general science from literally any college or university would be an appropriate foundation for this field. If an institution offers an environmental studies major, that too might be suitable if it is heavy in emphasis on science. Along the way, you should take as many management, statistics, and computer sciences courses as possible. You should aim, as soon as possible, for graduate school and get a master's degree. This might be a master's in public health administration, public administration, business administration, management, or one of the environmental sciences.

Where Would You Work as an Environmental Health Scientist?

Local, state, and federal government agencies employ the majority of environmental health scientists, in departments such as public health, environmental protection, conservation, and fish and wildlife services.

The armed forces offer some of the more attractive career opportunities in environmental health. Colleges and universities employ environmental health scientists to teach and do research. Industry has a growing number of environmental management departments and research laboratories where such personnel are in demand—in part, to keep up with the flow of paper needed to comply with the tremendous number of government regulations regarding health and safety.

At the Centers for Disease Control (CDC) in Atlanta, the Center for Environmental Health and Injury Control advertised in 1990 for mathematicians/statisticians, pharmacologists, and environmental health scientists. For example, CDC sought members for its Emergency Response Coordination Group, which provides a 24-hour service for consultation when disaster strikes. On standby are physicians, toxicologists, environmental health scientists, chemists, health physicists, epidemiologists, and emergency response coordinators. A team can be assembled within twenty minutes and dispatched anywhere in the world, as one was when the earthquake struck northern California in 1989. In between such disasters, the CDC staff develops contingency plans and develops computerized systems and data bases that are needed in emergencies.

This planning and program development takes place in conjunction with nonfederal agencies and the private sector.

The National Institute of Environmental Health Sciences—a component of the National Institutes of Health and headquartered at Research Triangle Park, North Carolina—recently issued an announcement that it was recruiting an epidemiologist/health scientist. Qualifications sought included:

> Successful completion of all requirements for a Ph.D. (or equivalent doctoral degree) in an academic field relating to epidemiology or the health sciences; or in lieu of the doctorate successful completion of a full four-year course of study leading to a bachelor's or higher degree, with major study in the field of health sciences; plus professional experience that, in combination with the bachelor's degree, is considered equivalent to the Ph.D. level.

The National Institute for Occupational Safety and Health—a component of CDC located in Cincinnati, Ohio—also employs environmental health scientists.

All the named government agencies, and others, have cooperative education, Presidential Management Intern, stay-in-school, and summer employment programs.

What Do Environmental Health Scientists Earn?

The announcements above were listed at the GS-13/14 levels. This means that someone meeting the qualifications at either level could be hired. The GS-13 level, in 1991, pays $44,092 per annum to start, and the GS-14, $52,104 to start. Each grade has ten steps, through which an employee may move upward annually, assuming a satisfactory annual job evaluation, to annual salaries of $57,322 and $67,737 respectively.

It is likely that beginning candidates, with bachelor's degrees and limited practical experience, would be offered GS-9 ($25,569) or, with one or two years experience, GS-11 ($30,937).

Salaries in industry would be somewhat higher.

What is the Job Future for Environmental Health Scientists?

This is another job area (like ecology) which the Bureau of Labor Statistics does not describe in its *Occupational Outlook Handbook.*

In the preceding chapter are a number of statements about the expected impact of biotechnology on job opportunities for biological scientists and environmental chemists. Similar assessments can be made, as well, for environmental health scientists. They are needed in the biotechnology industry—from the Department of Defense's biological warfare laboratories, to the Center for Disease Control's massive germ-containment laboratories, to industry's extensive clean-air compliance efforts.

According to *Healthy People 2000,* the Department of Health and Human Services forecasts that 121,000 additional environmental health specialists will be needed by the year 2000.

"Currently, there are only 1,500 environmental health graduates nationwide each year," according to the report. "As a result, government agencies are filling positions with inappropriately educated personnel . . . . Increasing the number of specialists in environmental health should be undertaken in conjunction with training in environmental health for physicians, generalists in medicine and engineering, and public school teachers."

The need is recognized; the barrier is in setting priorities and finding funding under tight budgetary constraints.

ENVIRONMENTAL MEDICINE

The category of *environmental medicine* consists of four different professionals, whose functions are in some ways similar to those of environmental health scientists but differ in one respect: They are the only professionals who can treat patients. The degrees, with the abbreviations that distinguish them, are:

Doctor of Medicine (M.D.)
Doctor of Osteopathy (D.O.)

Registered Nurse (R.N.)
Doctor of Veterinary Medicine (D.V.M.)

Any one of the four professionals listed could be in charge of a particular environmental health team for disease control, laboratory research, or field studies; which one would be in charge would depend upon which individual was senior and had the expertise to deal with the problems confronted.

THE ENVIRONMENTAL PHYSICIAN

Any physician is responsible for diagnosis, treatment, and prevention of disease, injury or other physical or mental condition of the human patient. Both M.D.'s and D.O.'s use all accepted methods of treatment. Osteopathic physicians (or osteopaths), however, believe particularly but not exclusively that the proper functioning of the musculoskeletal (muscle-bone) structure of the body is integral to the maintenance of the individual's overall health. In public health and preventive medicine, there are no differences in the qualifications or practice techniques between the two types of physicians.

The American Medical Association (AMA) is concerned, on behalf of its members, all of whom are physicians, about a host of environmental health matters. Its latest statement of policies and issues of concern on environmental, public, and occupational health runs to twenty-three pages.

Among the issues on which the AMA's House of Delegates has taken positions are agent orange/dioxin, AIDS/HIV virus, air pollution, alcohol and driving, asbestos, athletic training, automobile injuries, automobile safety, biological warfare programs, boxing, confidentiality of occupational medical records, drug use by athletes, drug testing of employees, emergency planning, employees' right to know (about workplace health hazards), energy health risks and nuclear energy, environmental stewardship, fire protection, flame-resistant apparel, fluoridation of public water supplies, formaldehyde, global climate change and the greenhouse effect, handguns, immunization, infant mortality, infectious medical waste, ionizing radiation, lead, ozone, pesticides, pollution control, radiation emergencies, radioactive wastes, radon, sanitary facilities for agricultural workers, smallpox vaccination, snuff and chewing tobacco, sports medicine, tobacco smoking, venereal (sexually-transmitted) disease, water pollution, and workers' reproduction rights.

What Do Environmental Physicians Do?

Many physicians emerge from the long course of education and training—eight to ten years or more beyond high school, the longest regimen of any profession—challenged by the opportunity not just to *treat* disease, but to *prevent* it. They may have been idealistic to begin with. Something then may have happened to push them in the direction of preventive medicine and public health. It could have been exposure to a charismatic professor, experience in working with the poor in a slum clinic, a stint in the uniformed services, an overseas internship, or an assignment in the Peace Corps or the Indian Health Service of the Public Health Service. Preventive medicine and public health (environmental health) is one of twenty-six specialty areas from which the M.D. may choose; there are sixteen specialties available to the D.O.

What Education Would You Need to Become an Environmental Physician?

Basic education—four years of college and four years of medical school—is required of all physicians, regardless of later specialization. Specialty training may take an additional two to five years or more.

The high school student aiming for premed and med school takes about what any science major would take—math, science, English, speech, and social studies. In college, one continues with advanced courses in all those subjects, plus physics, basic calculus, biology, organic and inorganic chemistry, and one or two languages.

Medicine is *the* most difficult profession to enter. It enjoys the highest prestige and the highest level of remuneration of almost any calling, so it attracts the brightest students with outstanding secondary school records. Competition for limited slots in freshman classes is extremely keen. If you aim for a career in medicine, aim high and aim early. At about the junior year in college, you must take a medical college preadmissions test. (See your counselor about arrangements to take it, as well as about meeting the other qualifications for admission to medical school.)

The medical-school curriculum includes anatomy, pharmacology, biochemistry, physiology, microbiology, and pathology, plus clinical subjects such as pediatrics, radiology, obstetrics-gynecology, and internal medicine. Laboratory and clinical training are increasingly integrated throughout the four years.

All states require a license to practice medicine. Additional specialty training may be required. To conduct research or to administer programs, a license is not required, but many researchers and administrators with healing arts degrees choose to be licensed.

Environmental medicine is particularly rich in the resources available for lifelong learning. This specialist may choose, usually after a few years of practice, to attend a school of public health for the Master of Public Health (M.P.H.) or Doctor of Public Health (D.P.H.) degree. The purpose of this additional education might be primarily to acquire new scientific skills. It might be to become better qualified to teach public health methodology. Or it might be to learn to manage a complex program (something medical school does not teach). Of course it might be all three things together.

Where Would You Work as an Environmental Physician?

The environmental physician may be full-time, working on the staff of a corporation or public health agency, or part-time, maintaining a private practice in addition.

In a corporation, the function might be called occupational or industrial medicine. In a state or local health department, the physician might or might not see patients, administer shots, teach in a medical school, or lecture on health matters to school or community groups.

If part-time, the physician might spend a day or half-day a week operating a clinic, either general or specialized—for example, taking care of patients with acquired immunodeficiency syndrome, or AIDS—

giving shots, testing children for high blood lead levels, or advising on the risks of waterborne disease or toxic agents. Part-time environmental physicians normally are internists or are in one of the internal medicine specialties—cardiology, infectious diseases, gastroenterology, and oncology, among others.

If full-time, the physician might practice clinical medicine to some extent, or might be completely occupied by managerial or administrative tasks. The post likely would be on the staff of a local or state health department; and in a large department its occupant would specialize in one program. This program might involve any of the diseases or specialties already mentioned, such as AIDS; women's, maternal, and child health; or infectious diseases.

At the federal level, this physician might be one of the renowned "disease detectives" of the Centers for Disease Control in Atlanta. These investigators keep their bags packed, ready to fly on a moment's notice, anywhere in the nation or the world, to help quell mysterious disease outbreaks, which often are associated with the physical environment. Examples are legionnaire's disease and toxic shock syndrome.

Some environmental physicians teach at schools of medicine or public health. Many retire to lucrative jobs in industrial medicine, pharmaceutical research or testing, clinical medicine, product development, toxicology, or other private-sector endeavors. Others expand, or take up, private practice, either in the places where they have worked or in Sun Belt retirement areas.

What Do Environmental Physicians Earn?

Half-million-dollar incomes are not unusual for private practitioners in well-to-do communities—but not for physicians in public health. The physician who goes into public health is motivated to serve in this way—at a sacrifice—for all physicians come up through the same route, with the same expenses.

The *Occupational Outlook Handbook* states, ''A physician's training is costly . . . . While education costs have increased, student financial assistance has not. Scholarships, while still available, have become harder to find. Loans are available, but subsidies to reduce interest rates are limited.''

After the four years in medical school come three years of residency, for which allowances of $24,000 to $31,000 a year are common. Many hospitals also provide full or partial room and board, but the total is not munificent. Additional years are required for specialty training. Finally, there may be the high expense of buying or relocating a practice or opening an office. This financial investment will vary according to the equipment required by the specialty—relatively low for a psychiatrist, high for a radiologist.

All of this could add up to half a million dollars before the physician can even dream of a club membership or a Mercedes. During the first year or two of independent practice, many physicians barely pay expenses. As a rule, however, their earnings rise rapidly as their practice develops.

According to the American Medical Association's Center for Health Policy Research:

> [The] average income after expenses, for all physicians was about $132,300 in 1987; those under 36 years of age averaged $96,100. Earnings vary according to specialty; the number of years in practice; geographic region; hours worked; and the physician's skill, personality, and professional reputation. Self-employed physicians—those who own or are part owners of their medical practice—had an average income of $146,200, while those who were employed by others earned an average of $99,600 a year.

Top government salaries are competitive, but top openings come up infrequently.

One civil service position advertised in 1990 was in the Senior Executive Service (SES), with a base salary up to $81,700 per year. SES members are eligible for various bonuses and awards, and physicians are eligible for a comparability allowance of up to $20,000 per year. Total compensation could be approximately $110,000 per year.

The Department of Veterans Affairs (VA) operates the free world's largest health-care system, with 172 hospitals, 233 outpatient clinics, and 119 nursing homes. VA employs 13,000 full- or part-time staff physicians, who in turn supervise the more than 30,000 residents who rotate through VA hospitals each year. Another 28,000 private, community-based physicians provide fee-based care in VA facilities. Salaries in the VA vary according to experience, specialty, board certification, and supervisory level. Ads in the *Journal of the American Medical Association* for environmental medicine specialists at VA hospitals offered salaries in 1990 of $60,000 to $70,000, plus the comparability allowance amounting to another $10,000 to $20,000.

What Is the Job Future for Environmental Physicians?

The Bureau of Labor Statistics expects overall employment of physicians—in private practice and other settings—to grow faster than the average for all occupations through the year 2000. Factors influencing that prediction include population growth and aging; continued introduction of new treatments and procedures; and the widespread ability to pay for services through private insurance, Medicare, and Medicaid. However, "the need to replace physicians is low because almost all physicians remain in the profession until they must retire," i.e., instead of retiring after twenty or twenty-five years, the physician frequently remains in practice for forty or forty-five years. (The threat of malpractice suits and the cost of malpractice insurance are beginning to hold down that curve, and we are seeing more physicians retiring earlier than we did prior to the 1990s.)

During the 1970s the number of medical school graduates rose substantially—"a deliberate, publicly subsidized response to the perceived shortage of medical personnel," says the BLS. "If the number of medical school graduates remains at current high levels, the supply of physicians is expected to exceed demand. Some communities may have too many physicians, leading to fewer patient visits per physician and correspondingly lower earnings."

There were about 535,000 physicians in the United States in 1988. According to American Medical Association figures, between five thousand and ten thousand were engaged in public health or occupational medicine.

Public support is building for expansion of public health programs. There is evidence that federal, professional-society, and corporate support is being mustered behind the 298 specific health objectives for the year 2000, described above under "Healthy People 2000." Also, there is strong support in Congress for a universal health care plan to cover the thirty-eight million Americans with no health insurance or inadequate health insurance. As such programs evolve, there will be a preventive medicine and public health component which inevitably will require more specialists, physicians included.

THE ENVIRONMENTAL NURSE

The nurse traditionally has been an important member of the public health team, serving in hospitals and clinics, in research laboratories, and out in the community, tracking and treating disease alongside the physician. He or she also long has been concerned with all the steps—immunizations, examinations, and inspection of the home and community—necessary to *prevent* the spread of communicable and infectious disease. A good bit of the credit for taking the vaccines, medicines, and education to people wherever they live goes to the public health nurse. Although the term *environmental nurse* is new, public health nurses traditionally have been concerned with improving environmental hygiene.

What Education Would You Need
to Become an Environmental Nurse?

There are about one thousand four hundred nursing programs available in the United States. In addition, more than one hundred universities offer master's degrees and several offer doctorates. Anyone interested in public health—the basic field of which environmental nursing is a part—should enroll in a bachelor's degree program (as opposed to the majority of programs which have lower requirements). Public health agencies require a bachelor's degree but prefer a master's as well. All states require a license to practice.

The high school student aiming for a degree in nursing should take, through high school and college, the same type of curriculum described above for the environmental physician. Similar resources for lifelong learning are available to the nurse as well as to the physician.

Where Would You Work as an Environmental Nurse?

All of the statements made above for environmental physicians apply, as well, to environmental nurses.

What Do Environmental Nurses Earn?

Publicly employed nurses are among the highest paid in a traditionally low-paying profession. This does not mean that they have achieved equity with other professionals, but especially in the research or non-clinical agencies, they are respected members of the health team and are compensated accordingly.

Those entering the Public Health Service, for the limited openings at the National Institutes of Health or the Centers for Disease Control, in 1990 received starting salaries of $25,569 to $30,937 (GS-9/11), but master's degrees and/or one or more years experience are required at this level.

At the Department of Veterans Affairs, which employs 35,000 nurses, the 1991 budget called for adding almost 1,000 more, raising their salaries, and adjusting nurses' pay to compete with the scales prevailing in different communities. This could mean slightly higher salaries than in the Public Health Service, where most nurses are civil servants under a different system from the VA's. (Still a third system, in the PHS, is the commissioned officer corps; a small number of nurses in management hold commissions, with different salaries and benefits from those in the civil service.)

At the local level, public health nurses make 10 to 20 percent less than at the federal level (but lower living expenses may compensate for lower salaries).

Public agencies, like hospitals and nursing homes, are faced with a continuing shortage of nurses. Many are responding with flexible work schedules, child care, educational benefits, bonuses, shared decisionmaking, and other incentives designed to retain existing staff and to attract licensed nurses who may be employed elsewhere or are currently inactive.

What is the Job Future for Environmental Nurses?

A small number of the 1.6 million registered nurses in the United States qualify as public health nurses—and fewer still as specialists in environmental nursing. Yet, many subtle factors would seem to contribute to a bright future for this component of nursing. Increasing public and political interest is being directed toward public health and environmental protection, maternal and child health, and community medicine and health education. Emerging are such women's-health issues as reproductive rights in the workplace, abortion and fetal rights, research using fetal tissue, breast cancer, women and AIDS, and greater inclusion of women in studies on the epidemiology and control of cancer and heart disease.

By the year 2000, nine million veterans, or 37 percent of the veteran population, will be age sixty-five or older. Even now, millions of veterans are dependent on nursing services, often in the community. The rising incidence of Alzheimer's disease and other geriatric problems is putting new demands on the VA's physicians, nurses, and social workers.

Agencies are spending more and more each year to recruit nurses, through advertising, job fairs, bonuses to employees who recruit other nurses, and special incentives. Short-term appointments enable nurses to winter in the Sun Belt and summer in the northern tier of states, or wherever they choose. Ads in the *Nation's Health,* the monthly newspaper of the American Public Health Association, increasingly specify "Master of Public Health or Master of Science in Nursing required" for teaching, administrative, or research positions.

None of this tells us how many public health nurses there are, nor does it predict how many will be needed this decade or the next. Reliable studies are yet to be announced.

THE PUBLIC HEALTH VETERINARIAN

The veterinarian whose practice is most intimately connected to environmental management is the *public health veterinarian.*

In the words of the American Veterinary Medical Association's careers booklet:

> Today's veterinarian is dedicated to protecting the health and welfare of both animals and people.
>
> Veterinarians are highly educated and skilled in preventing, diagnosing, and treating animal health problems . . .
>
> In taking the veterinarian's oath, the doctor solemnly swears to use her or his scientific knowledge and skills "for the benefit of society, through the protection of animal health, the relief of animal suffering, the conservation of livestock resources, the promotion of public health, and the advancement of medical knowledge."

What Do Public Health Veterinarians Do?

Public health veterinarians are directly concerned with the promotion of public health and the advancement of knowledge, but that does not explain what they do. Simply put, what they do is intervene and interrupt the transmission of disease from animals to humans.

There are some forty diseases to which humans are prone, and in the transmission of which animals play some role. Such a disease is called a *zoonosis,* defined by the American Public Health Association as "An infection or infectious disease transmissible under natural conditions from vertebrate animals to man."

The most dreaded such disease is rabies because it is almost invariably fatal if not treated immediately. This acute viral infection most often is transmitted from rabid dogs, foxes, skunks, and raccoons, among other biting animals. Vampire and fruit-eating bats of Central and South America are infected with the rabies virus—but rarely are the source of human infections. When anyone is bitten by an animal suspected of being infected, the animal, if available, should be killed and examined for rabies. If rabies is determined—or if the animal cannot be caught for examination—the victim must be vaccinated as soon as possible after the bite and revaccinated four more times, then observed by a physician for at least ninety days.

Anthrax, to take another example, may be transmitted through the skin from contact with contaminated hair, wool, hides, and manufactured products containing those substances.

Certain types of food poisoning may be acquired by eating products containing frozen or dried eggs contaminated with salmonella. Q fever is an airborne infection sometimes suffered by veterinarians, dairy workers, and farmers. Psittacosis is called "parrot fever," and it strikes those who work around birds. Several forms of encephalitis can be transmitted by mosquitoes from horses to humans. Rocky Mountain spotted fever is transmitted by ticks. Trichinosis, whose infectious agent resides in swine, is transmitted through eating infected pork.

Usually, veterinarians in public health conduct programs of intervention, stopping the transmission of disease from animals to humans. It is a very straightforward, scientific process. But sometimes, they use their knowledge of scientific medicine in activities in which animals play no role. In the *Occupational Outlook Handbook* we read:

> It is not generally understood that veterinarians contribute to human as well as animal health care. They may join physicians and scientists in carrying out research in, for example, cancer treatment; epidemiology or animal pathology; changing technology in food production, which present threats to food safety. Residues from herbicides, pesticides, and antibiotics used in food production pose a particular problem. Scientific advances in livestock production have, paradoxically, created a need for veterinarians capable of dealing with contamination of the food chain by toxic chemicals. Some veterinarians teach in veterinary colleges, work in zoos or animals laboratories, or engage in a combination of clinical and research activities.

What Education Would You Need to Become a Public Health Veterinarian?

There are twenty-seven accredited veterinary colleges in the United States. Each prescribes its own preveterinary admission requirements. Typically, these include basic language arts, social sciences, humanities, mathematics, chemistry, and the biological and physical sciences. Three years of college is the minimum required for admission.

In most colleges of veterinary medicine, the professional program is divided into two phases. During the first phase, the student takes preclinical sciences including anatomy, physiology, pathology, pharmacology, and microbiology. Most of the time is spent in classroom and laboratory study.

The second phase of professional study is largely clinical. Students work with animals and deal with owners who use the school's clinical services. The clinical curriculum includes courses on infectious and noninfectious diseases, advanced pathology, applied anatomy, obstetrics, radiology, clinical medicine, and surgery. Applied studies include public health, preventive medicine, toxicology, nutrition, professional ethics, and business practices.

A veterinary degree program is rigorous, requiring about four thousand hours programmed in classroom, laboratory, and clinical study. Because of this heavy schedule, the student must devote many additional hours at night and on weekends and holidays to reading assignments, library research, and independent study.

The program leads, at the end of four years, to award of the Doctor of Veterinary Medicine (D.V.M.) degree.

Where Would You Work as a Public Health Veterinarian?

The new veterinary graduate may qualify for a civilian job with the U.S. Department of Agriculture as a meat or poultry inspector, or for a commissioned corps appointment to the U.S. Public Health Service as an epidemiologist. Depending on the agency and the duties, a license from a state—any state—may be required.

The career public health veterinarian usually is employed by a unit of local, state, or federal government. As the basic veterinary medical education is rigorously scientific, many veterinarians become health administrators in programs remote from animal health. According to the Bureau of Labor Statistics, veterinarians held about forty-six thousand jobs in 1988. Most were in private practice. About two thousand were employed by the federal government, chiefly in the Departments of

Agriculture, Health and Human Services, and the Interior. An additional six hundred served in the military.

Other important employers of veterinarians are colleges of veterinary medicine and medical schools, research laboratories, livestock farms, animal food companies, pharmaceutical firms, and biotechnology companies.

With the emergence in the late 1980s of intensified concern over the ethical and humane treatment of animals in biological research, the public health veterinarian has found a new role: caretaker of and advocate for animals who live in research laboratory animal colonies and are used for experiments.

When a "zoonosis" is even remotely possible, veterinary epidemiologists on the staff of, or in training at, the Centers for Disease Control are among the "disease detectives" who investigate the outbreak.

A veterinarian can meet military requirements or make an interesting career serving in the veterinary corps of the Army or Air Force. One's functions in such service would usually relate to protection of the health of military personnel against the zoonoses described above. But they also could be general sanitation, research, or a hundred other functions indistinguishable from the general-science duties which might be performed by a Ph.D. or M.D. A veterinarian also can meet military requirements by service in the commissioned corps of the Public Health Service, most commonly at the Centers for Disease Control, described above, or assigned to a state or local health department.

Then there are some functions essential to public health protection which only the veterinarian is qualified or permitted by law to perform. You have noticed in the grocery ads, "Grade A Prime" or "Choice" meats advertised. A federal veterinarian certified that meat after inspecting it in the packing plant and labeled it to protect you against disease. Other veterinarians of the Department of Agriculture supervise the health of animals in stockyards, inspect poultry, enforce quarantine regulations, and monitor the export and import of animals and animal products. They assure the safety and quality of drugs used to treat animals, both to protect the human consumers of meat against communicable diseases and to protect the investment which farmers and others have in the animals' health. And they conduct research on, and supervise the licensing of, firms which manufacture serums and vaccines for animals. Interestingly, veterinarians also have a responsibility under federal law to monitor and assure that livestock are slaughtered as humanely and painlessly as possible.

Veterinarians in the Science and Education Administration of the U.S. Department of Agriculture participate in a wide range of research activities: to improve livestock (and poultry) productivity through improved breeding, feeding, and management practices and to develop methods for controlling animal diseases, and parasites and insect pests which affect livestock. In addition to basic and applied animal research, these scientists have new priorities such as research to develop energy technologies to reduce animal agriculture's dependence on fossil fuels. Veterinarians, among others, are confronted by such questions as: Can manure from various animal operations produce enough methane gas to supply nearby buildings with heat and electricity?

Much research of that type is conducted in federal laboratories and in cooperative experiment stations of the state colleges and universities. It also is conducted by other university staffs under federal contracts and grants. Hundreds of veterinarians, federal and otherwise, participate in these studies.

Veterinarians also are employed by the U.S. Food and Drug Administration to help protect consumers by assuring the safety and purity of drugs used to treat animals. Pharmaceutical and chemical companies employ veterinarians in research and testing. Private foundations engaged in medical, public health, food, and wildlife preservation activities around the world employ veterinarians for environmental programs.

What Do Public Health Veterinarians Earn?

Newly graduated veterinarians employed by the federal government start at GS-11 at a starting salary of $30,937 per annum. The average salary of veterinarians in federal service is $45,000.

According to limited data from the AVMA, the average net income for private practice veterinarians ranges between $50,000 and $60,000. Incomes can be assumed to vary considerably, depending on type of practice and geographic location.

What is the Job Future for Public Health Veterinarians?

Employment of veterinarians is expected to grow faster than average for all occupations through the year 2000. Contributing factors include growth in the animal population, emphasis on scientific methods of breeding and raising livestock and poultry, and continued support for public health and disease control programs.

The BLS regards the outlook as "extremely good" for public health veterinarians, especially with those who have pursued the master of public health or other postgraduate degree. Demand for specialists in toxicology, laboratory animal medicine, and pathology is expected to remain strong, as is the demand for faculty at colleges of veterinary medicine and other medical schools.

ENVIRONMENTAL SANITATION

If you are more interested in practical problems than in theory, better satisfied by helping people avoid trouble than in working at a laboratory bench, then consider becoming a *sanitarian*. (The sanitarian is not to be confused with the sanitary engineer, which is what environmental engineers traditionally were called and whose duties have been described in earlier pages.)

What Do Sanitarians Do?

The sanitarian traditionally has been responsible for interpreting and enforcing local, state, and federal laws, regulations, and standards—mostly local, it should be noted—respecting the sanitation of food, milk, water supply, garbage disposal, sewage disposal, and housing. Today, to those responsibilities has been added the stimulation of community action for better health through better environmental sanitation of all types. This means that the sanitarian promotes and helps secure such improvements as water supply extension, improved sewage disposal facilities, safer recreational areas, and more hygienic conditions in nursing and convalescent homes.

One level of duty is that of *inspector,* checking on the cleanliness of dairies, food processing plants, restaurants, and plant and hospital food services. As a sanitarian you would also visit schools, hotels and motels, swimming pools, parks, and certain types of housing to observe, make measurements, collect samples and specimens for laboratory analysis, and make recommendations regarding the facilities' compliance with public health and environmental protection and safety laws and regulations. Another level of duty is as *regulator,* citing violators of codes or even closing them down.

A third level of duty for the senior sanitarian is as *manager.* You would then develop and manage programs to prevent contamination, control insects and rodents, manage disposal of wastes, and insure adequate water supplies. You might also plan for emergency disaster aid, teach health education classes, speak before community groups, and work with the county agent on agricultural sanitation problems such as disposal of animal and vegetable wastes.

A *supervising sanitarian* plans and directs environmental health programs and may supervise a large staff. Sanitarians at all levels serve the public as educators and interpreters. They provide consultation to owners, operators, and employees of businesses; to contractors; to school, government, and elected officials; and to any citizens who wish to pose questions or requests. They may draft proposed laws and regulations. They may give expert testimony in court cases involving alleged violations of such laws and regulations. They may serve as arbitrators in quasi-judicial proceedings. With the recent emergence of new and more complex pollution problems, especially those involving toxic wastes and hazardous substances, the sanitarian can expect to be called on far more frequently, by all the parties named, for expert advice and counsel.

What Education Would You Need to Become a Sanitarian?

A bachelor's degree in biology, chemistry, general engineering, or environmental sciences generally is acceptable for an entry job as sanitarian. In most states one cannot practice as a professional sanitarian without a bachelor's degree. More than sixty colleges and universities offer a bachelor's degree in environmental health (or sanitation), which requires a minimum of thirty semester hours in the physical or biological sciences. The communications and liberal arts courses mentioned so frequently in connection with other professions are stressed. A typical curriculum's core courses would include microbiology (bacteriology), biostatistics, epidemiology, environmental sciences, administration, and field work.

A graduate degree is not offered in sanitation as such, but sanitarians frequently take graduate work, through the master's level and sometimes the doctorate, in science, public health, management, or some other field.

The National Environmental Health Association (NEHA) awards an option of three credentials to members who meet educational and experiential requirements and may need to complete examinations. They are (a) Certified Hazardous Waste Specialist (CHWS), developed under a grant from the Environmental Protection Agency, and which requires a bachelor's degree with major course work in the sciences or in environmental health; (b) Registered Environmental Health Specialist (REHS), required by state registration boards, which has as prerequisites a bachelor's degree and a minimum of two years' environmental health experience; and (c) Environmental Health Technician (EHT), which is in increasing demand for positions in the military and which requires a high school diploma and a minimum of two years' environmental health experience or an associate's degree in a related field.

NEHA, with support from the Environmental Protection Agency and the Public Health Service, has developed seventeen self-paced learning modules for the individual's continuing education. These modules cover such topics as water quality, wastewater treatment, air pollution, injury and disease prevention, noise control, data management, and communications.

Where Would You Work as a Sanitarian?

Three out of four sanitarians work for the federal, state, or local governments. Another group works for producers and processors of food and dairy products. Others teach, consult, or work for hospitals, trade associations or for such firms as insurance companies. Because of their broad background in environmental sciences, such people readily move back and forth between the private and public sectors. With added educational and experiential qualifications, they may seek steady advancement and new challenges.

What Do Sanitarians Earn?

According to the Bureau of Labor Statistics, health and regulatory inspectors, including sanitarians, start at around $16,000. That would be equivalent to a GS-5 grade, where step 1 carries a beginning salary of $16,875.

The chances for advancement are good, and by mid-career one could easily be making $40,000 to $50,000 per year.

Government sanitarians come into contact with owners of businesses and executives of such companies at food processors. They may be offered jobs by these contacts, and in changing jobs improve their salaries by 50 percent or more.

What Is the Job Future for Sanitarians?

At the same time that the duties of the sanitarian have broadened, the number of businesses which must be inspected has expanded. Think of the rapid growth that you have observed of restaurants, shopping malls, and fast-food places.

The emerging genetic engineering and biotechnology industries have been mentioned previously, in Chapters 3 and 4. Some research in these areas requires operations to be conducted in a germ-free environment. For example, the Centers for Disease Control, at its headquarters in Atlanta, has a large germ-free containment building for safely storing and studying the agents of anthrax, rabies, smallpox, and other deadly infectious agents. Sanitarians are among the specialists who helped design and who operate the facility.

As the BLS does not include sanitarians as a category in the *Occupational Outlook Handbook,* there are no ''official'' projections as to the job future for sanitarians. The author's own studies indicate that growth to the year 2000 will be steady, fueled by the biotechnology industry, the expansion of Superfund, the hazardous waste industry, and, hopefully, expansion of the economy.

HEALTH PHYSICS

What Do Health Physicists Do?

The *health physicist* (alternatively, *radiological physicist* or *radiobiologist*) is responsible for the health aspects of radiation. This is the professional who is concerned with the design, testing, maintenance, and operation of X-ray machines and related radiation equipment. This professional works with radioactive materials, nuclear reactors, and particle accelerators. He or she takes measurements of environmental radioactive backgrounds, natural or man-made.

What Education Would You Need to Become a Health Physicist?

A bachelor's degree in physics is sufficient to qualify one to an entry job as a health physicist. Courses in chemistry, biology, and computer sciences are essential. A master's degree with emphasis on statistics would be helpful.

The American Board of Health Physics certifies professionals as C.H.P.'s (certified health physicists) when they meet prerequisites and pass an examination.

Where Would You Work as a Health Physicist?

Since the accidents at Three Mile Island and at Chernobyl in the Soviet Union, this nation's nuclear health and safety program has been considerably augmented. The Nuclear Regulatory Commission, as a consequence, is a major employer of health physicists. Another is the U.S. Department of Energy, both on federal jobs and indirectly through the contractors who run the national laboratories such as Argonne, Brookhaven, Oak Ridge, Los Alamos, and Hanford. Another category of employer is hospitals and medical research institutions which use X-rays and radiation for therapy. Health physicists also are employed by state and local health and environmental protection departments. In the private sector, the manufacturers of radiation equipment, power companies, and consulting firms also employ considerable numbers.

What Do Health Physicists Earn?

According to the Bureau of Labor Statistics, health physicists with bachelor's degrees and no prior experience start in the federal government at about the GS-7 level, paying a beginning salary of $20,902. With a master's degree and/or some experience, one could expect to enter government service at the GS-9 level, paying $25,569 to start.

Chances for advancement are good, and by mid-career one can expect to be making from $44,000 to $52,000. The work brings the health physicist into contact with many industrial managers, contacts which could lead to job offers at substantially higher salaries.

What Is the Job Future for Health Physicists?

After energy conservation caused a slowing of demand for electricity in the mid-1970s, power companies cancelled many contracts for nuclear reactors and halted work on plants under construction. After Three Mile Island, the public protests against nuclear power siting and the enormous burden of down-time costs—$1 million or more per day that a plant is not in operation—even power enthusiasts took a second look at nuclear energy. All such factors are having inhibiting effects on nuclear programs.

More and more health physicists are required to meet the health and safety regulations for those plants which remain in operation. Various electronic devices are coming into ever more widespread use, too: microwave ovens in homes and restaurants, elaborate CAT scanners (for rapid, accurate diagnosis of tumors) in hospitals, and a variety of radiation instruments in plants and laboratories. The Superfund and hazardous waste management programs are major contributors to growing demand for health physicists.

INDUSTRIAL HYGIENE

What Do Industrial Hygienists Do?

Become an *industrial hygienist* and, as the title indicates, you would work in or with industry. You would conduct activities to eliminate if possible, or at least to control, occupational health hazards and diseases. Concerns include: (a) chemical stresses such as dust or gas; (b) physical stresses such as radiation or noise; (c) biological factors including insects and fungi; and (d) ergonomic (that is, work-related) stresses such as monotony and work pressure.

Many specialists are trying to anticipate the potential cancer, birth defects, mental retardation, emphysema, black lung disease, and mental illnesses which might result in the years ahead from stresses and impacts in the workplace today. The industrial hygienist is the key professional who can take immediate, practical steps to tighten standards, remove hazards, and ban toxic substances whenever they are identified. These steps alleviate short-term illness and contribute to long-term worker health.

What Education Would You Need
to Become an Industrial Hygienist?

The basic educational requirement for industrial hygiene is a college degree with a major in engineering or one of the physical sciences. A few technological universities offer degrees, but most professionals are graduates of other institutions with a major or minor in engineering or science. Industrial hygienists frequently take a master's degree in industrial management or public administration.

Where Would You Work as an Industrial Hygienist?

The industrial hygienist may work in industry, a consulting firm, a governmental regulatory agency, or in another arrangement. The Labor Department's Occupational Safety and Health Administration, for instance, employs about six hundred industrial hygienists or other health scientists. Others are to be found in the occupational health department of a manufacturing company or with an insurance company holding workers' compensation policies for a number of companies with multiple plants. Or it might be a transportation company such as an airline, public utility, mining operation, labor union, or consulting company serving many clients. Still other companies are in genetic engineering and biotechnology.

What Do Industrial Hygienists Earn?

According to the Occupational Safety and Health Administration, Department of Labor, it employs industrial hygienists at entry-level GS-5, paying a beginning salary of $16,875. OSHA is the regulatory agency.

Another agency sets the standards and conducts the research on which standards are set. This is the National Institute of Occupational Safety and Health (NIOSH), which is part of the Centers for Disease Control. NIOSH, based in Cincinnati, Ohio, also employs industrial hygienists at the same entry level.

At this writing, another component of CDC, its Center for Environmental Health at Atlanta, is recruiting for industrial hygienists with a minimum of three years of experience or graduate education. This is at the GS-12 level, paying a starting salary of $37,079.

What Is the Job Future for Industrial Hygienists?

It appears that there were about two thousand industrial hygienists in the mid-1970s, a population which has doubled to four thousand today, and is expected to rise another 50 percent, to six thousand by the mid-1990s.

WHERE SHOULD YOU WRITE FOR MORE INFORMATION?

Air & Waste Management Association
  Three Gateway Center
  Pittsburgh, Pa. 15230

American Industrial Hygiene Council
  475 Wolf Ledges Parkway
  Akron, Ohio 44331

American Medical Association
  Division of Biomedical Sciences
  515 North State Street
  Chicago, Ill. 60610

American Osteopathic Association
  212 East Ohio Street
  Chicago, Ill. 60611

American Public Health Association
  1015 15th Street, N.W.
  Washington, D.C. 20005

American Society of Civil Engineers
  345 East 47th Street
  New York, N.Y. 10017

American Veterinary Medical Association
  930 North Meacham Road
  Schaumburg, Ill. 60196

American Water Works Association
  6666 West Qunicy Street
  Denver, Colo. 80235

Junior Engineering Technical Society
  1420 King Street, Suite 405
  Alexandria, Va. 22314-2715

National Association of Environmental Professionals
  P.O. Box 15210
  Alexandria, Va. 22309-0210

National Environmental Health Association
  720 South Colorado Boulevard
  Denver, Colo. 80222

National Safety Council
  Environmental Health Center
  1050 17th Street, N.W., Suite 770
  Washington, D.C. 20036

Water Pollution Control Federation
  601 Wythe Street
  Alexandria, Va. 22314

CHAPTER 5

NATURAL RESOURCES

The forest resources of our country are already seriously depleted. They can be renewed and maintained only by the co-operation of the forester and the practical man of business.—President Theodore Roosevelt in 1903

PROFESSIONS COVERED

Agricultural Sciences, Fisheries Conservation, Forestry, Range Management, Soil Conservation, Wildlife Conservation

President Teddy Roosevelt chose as the first chief forester of the nation Gifford Pinchot (1865–1946). In so doing, the President acknowledged the need for professionals in high positions to make conservation policy and to administer conservation programs. Pinchot, you see, was the first American to hold a degree in forestry. His philosophy was "Conservation means the wise *use* of the earth and its resources." (Italics added.) Poet John Muir (1838–1914), on the other hand, believed with Henry David Thoreau (1817–1860) that, "In Wildness is the *preservation* of the World." Thus, Pinchot and Muir became the symbolic leaders of opposing camps—users vs. preservers—which have been engaged in frequent conflict since the twentieth century began.

A notable early environmental controversy arose in 1901. It concerned development of a water supply for the city of San Francisco, which proposed to create a reservoir in the spectacularly scenic Hetch-Hetchy Valley in Yosemite National Park. Other sites were available, at higher cost. The question was whether an artificial impoundment should be allowed within a national park simply because it was more economical to build on that site than on others available. (The environmental impact statement process was designed, seventy years later, to weigh alternatives like this.)

Pitted on opposite sides of the controversy were Muir, the founder of the Sierra Club, who fervently believed in wilderness inviolate, and Pinchot, the first professional forester in America, who favored the Hetch-Hetchy Reservoir as a sensible use of resources. The economic argument carried the day, and Congress in 1913 approved the reservoir plan.

THE PROGRESSIVE MOVEMENT TO THE NEW DEAL

The Progressive Movement led by President Theodore Roosevelt during his two terms, 1901–1909, introduced the first official concern for conservation into public policy-making. Roosevelt was both prodded and publicized by the reform journalists, called "muckrakers," and was guided and assisted in conservation matters by Pinchot, his chief forester. Together, they started two dozen irrigation or reclamation projects and added more than 125 million acres to the national forest system. President Roosevelt also sponsored a White House Conference on Conservation in 1909 to which he sent invitations, personally delivered by Pinchot, to the Prime Minister of Canada and the President of Mexico.

Birdwatchers, fishers, hikers, hunters, naturalists, and others who loved the outdoors—joined by scientists—developed the concept of wildlife sanctuaries. They convinced legislators to institute hunting and fishing licenses to help pay for wildlife protection. And they worked zealously to protect local forests, marshes, and mountains from destruction. Except for their little-known efforts, the Grand Canyon, Yellowstone's geysers, the California giant sequoias, Florida's Everglades, Georgia's Golden Isles, and Massachusetts's Cape Cod, among hundreds of other natural and historic treasures, could have been destroyed by now.

Another President Roosevelt—Franklin Delano—made conservation of the land a keystone of his four terms. Between 1933 and 1942, more than two million young men, most of them previously unemployed, worked in the Civilian Conservation Corps (CCC) on a variety of outdoor restoration projects. They planted windbreaks on the Great Plains, started tree farms in the southeast, and hewed fire breaks across the Green Mountains of Vermont and the Sierra Nevadas of California.

BEHIND THE MODERN ENVIRONMENTAL MOVEMENT

After World War II, Americans were more conscious of the beauty and value of the land than ever before. In the 1940s and 1950s, several popular books brought environmental issues to widespread attention. Occasionally citizens mobilized to save and protect an environmental treasure. In the early 1950s, the Bureau of Reclamation decided that a dam should be built on the Green River at Echo Park, part of the Dinosaur National Monument in Colorado and Utah—Hetch-Hetchy all over again. This time the results were different. Wilderness preservationists, defensive about the sanctity of the national park and monument system, conducted a vigorous and successful campaign which brought the development to a halt in 1956.

During the 1950s, public demand for outdoor recreation was accelerating, and conflicts over finite recreation resources increasing. In 1958 Congress responded by establishing a commission to plan to meet recreation needs in America over the next forty years. President John F. Kennedy received its report in 1962, and his successor, President Lyndon B. Johnson, implemented many of its recommendations. Prodded by his wife, Lady Bird, Johnson viewed the environment as embracing beauty as well as utility. In 1965 he sponsored a White House Conference on the order of Teddy Roosevelt's conference of 1909. An unprecedented wave of citizen action followed.

Rachel Carson's *Silent Spring* (1962) was mentioned in Chapter 1. An arm of the White House established an expert committee on pesticides to scientifically study the issues Carson had raised, and its report largely vindicated her by recommending that many of her suggestions be made national policy.

On March 18, 1967, a tanker ran aground on Seven Stone Reef off England's southern coast. The resulting oil spill inflicted great damage on marine life and on the beaches of England and France.

That accident in Europe caused the U.S. Government to make contingency plans to cope with the spillage of oil or hazardous substances off its shores. Those plans proved invaluable when, on January 28, 1969, an oil well in the Santa Barbara, California, harbor blew, discharging enormous quantities of oil into the Pacific Ocean. Within three days oil covered nearly two hundred square miles of ocean and began washing up on beaches for hundred of miles. Without all types of communications media, especially color television, the impact on public opinion in this country might have been negligible. Millions of viewers, however, were moved by pictures of thousands of seabirds struggling to survive their coatings of oil and dispersing chemicals and were struck by the valiant efforts of volunteers trying to clean and save them. (Almost twenty years later, in 1988, an even greater spill followed the grounding, in Alaskan waters, of the *Exxon Valdez*. There followed the most extensive environmental cleanup ever attempted.)

It is ironic that oil spills still regularly occur, particularly because Santa Barbara was the symbolic trigger for the first Earth Day, which launched the modern environmental movement that now has reached worldwide proportions.

In this chapter we are concerned with natural resources, their enjoyment and diverse uses, from food and fiber to forests and fishes.

AGRICULTURAL SCIENCES

American agriculture is the most efficient in the world. Per capita, it is the most productive segment of our economy. Credit for American agriculture's accomplishments goes largely to the land grant colleges and universities with their network of cooperative state research and extension services. (There is no denying the contributions of technology and economies of scale, as small farms have been consolidated into more efficient large farming operations. In this respect, agriculture is similar to the industrial and marketing sectors, where expansion, mergers and absentee ownership characterize the business world.)

American agriculture is changing in response to changing social needs and demands. Its overdependence on chemicals is being questioned by environmentalists, and many farmers are moving into integrated pest control, using insecticides as little as possible. Early in the 1980s, organic farming was being promoted, for the first time, by the U.S. Department of Agriculture, and thousands of farmers were adopting its principles. Farmers were widely adopting new techniques of energy conservation in agriculture, at the same time making a growing contribution to energy supply through increased production of grain for alcohol that can be combined with gasoline to produce "gasohol."

The Bureau of Labor Statistics estimates that agriculture employs more than three million persons. For our purposes, we group together the scientific, technical, and professional occupations dealing with agriculture, its products, or the farm population, and call their practitioners *agriculture scientists*. The field includes:

- Those who conduct research on the production, distribution, and use of crops and animals for food and fiber. They may work at colleges of agriculture, cooperative research stations, in "agribusiness," or for other federal, state, or private agencies.
- Those who formally teach the agricultural sciences at land grant colleges and universities or other institutions offering agricultural studies.
- Those who do educational work in fields such as agricultural production and home economics and may conduct educational programs through youth groups such as the 4-H clubs. These are the *county agents* and *home economists* engaged in *extension* work, a cooperative effort of federal, state, and local governments which has had enormous impact on American agriculture and the lives of all Americans for more than a century. Hundreds of thousands of volunteers, including youth, further extend this outreach to provide services to millions of Americans, urban as well as rural.

The U.S. Department of Agriculture's Science and Education Administration operates eight major research centers and more than 150 other research facilities, located in virtually all the states. In addition, it sponsors research in hundreds of colleges.

Federally sponsored research and development embrace conservation and management of such natural resources as soil, water, and forests; animal and crop production-protection; crop utilization and postharvest technology; human nutrition and family-resource management; and domestic and export marketing.

Become an agricultural scientist and you might study the effects of changing climate and weather on agricultural production; work to eliminate the sources of pollution that result from agricultural practices; explore uses of fuel made from plant products; search for ways to reduce the use of fossil fuels in producing crops and livestock; test the possibilities of aquaculture (farming systems for plants and animals that live in water); find safe, feasible ways to use organic wastes; explore biological (nonchemical) pest control methods; promote urban and agricultural integrated pest management practices; develop methods for assuring the safety and quality of food and food products; conduct basic and applied research in the animal and plant sciences; do controlled experiments in human nutrition and diet; develop community resources in rural areas; conduct home audits for energy conservation; and develop systems to assist the public in coping with natural disaster emergencies.

What Do Agricultural Scientists Do?

- The *agricultural chemist* conducts research to improve crop yield and promote soil conservation; develops chemical compounds to control insects, weeds, fungi, and rodents; and experiments to determine proper usage of fertilizers or to investigate the problems of nitrogen fixation in soils.
- The *agricultural economist* deals with problems related to production, financing, pricing, and marketing of farm products; cost-benefit analyses for evaluating agricultural programs; and the effects of new technology on the supply of, and demand for, agricultural products.

- The *agricultural engineer* designs agricultural machinery and equipment and develops methods that will improve the production, processing, and distribution of food and numerous other agricultural products.
- The *agronomist* conducts experiments in field crop problems, develops new methods of growing crops to increase yields and to improve quality, and studies the effect of climates on crop production. The *horticulturist* works in a sub-specialty of agronomy with orchard and garden plants—trees for shade, fruit, and nuts; vegetables; and flowers—and the utilization of plant communities for the beautification of human communities.
- The *animal physiologist* studies the functions of various parts of the bodies of livestock, whereas the *animal scientist* is concerned with the production and management of farm animals, as in the selection, breeding, feeding, and marketing of farm animals; their housing, sanitation, and nutrition; and parasite and disease control. The *veterinarian* (already discussed in Chapter 4) is responsible for maintaining animal health and treating animal disease (and may work with animal physiologists and animal scientists in research).
- The *entomologist* concentrates on insects that injure plants and animals at any stage of their growth and development; this includes developing new pesticides that are less harmful to humans and less persistent in the biosphere than are the organic chemicals and developing integrated pest management practices, especially nonchemical methods.
- The *food chemist* may specialize in one kind of food, say, dairy products or cereals. (See Chapter 3 for description of the environmental chemist.)
- The *geneticist* develops strains, varieties, breeds, and hybrids of plants and animals that are better suited for food and fiber than those previously available.
- The *microbiologist* studies bacteria and other microorganisms to better understand their relation to human, animal, and plant health. The microbiologist also is the key scientist involved in the development and production of alcohols, amino acids, antibiotics, sugars, and vitamins.

- The *nutritionist* is concerned with how the body utilizes foods and nutrients, and the relation of those substances to human health and disease. The *human nutritionist* works on problems of human health, food, and the social, economic, and cultural aspects of peoples' diets, while the *animal nutritionist* works on the diet of livestock or domestic animals.
- The *plant pathologist* studies the causes of plant diseases.
- The *plant physiologist* studies the structure of plants and factors such as respiration, metabolism, and reproduction that affect growth.
- Finally, the *rural sociologist* (a social, not a physical, scientist) is concerned with the structure and functions of rural human society, from the individual through farm families, to the institutions of their isolated and not-so-isolated rural communities.

What Education Would You Need to Become an Agricultural Scientist?

Many agricultural science professions can be entered with only the bachelor's degree, sometimes with a major in environmental studies, especially one from a college of agriculture and natural resources.

One of the fastest-growing areas of higher education—as a direct consequence of the environmental movement—is colleges of agriculture and natural resources. During the 1980s, when college enrollments generally were dropping and many schools began recruiting students, the nation's agricultural colleges had all the students they could accommodate. That was attributable to a number of factors:

1. Young persons are motivated toward environmental careers because of their concerns for the environment, and colleges of agriculture broadened their curricula to become "environmental universities."
2. Young persons see the connections between and among environment, agriculture, food, health, and standards of living.
3. The new environmental universities offer *interdisciplinary/integrated/involved* studies to match the career interests and demands of young persons and their ideals.

4. This kind of education goes along with other interests of young persons such as "the new ruralism," defined as the population migration from the cities and suburbs to rural areas, and from the urban centers of the East Coast to the warmer, cleaner, less-crowded counties of the Sun Belt, the southern tier of states westward from Florida to California.

5. Finally, least tangible of all, there are things that make many people happy, and one is isolation—or at least distance from large numbers of fellow human beings. Living and/or working on a farm also provides satisfactions to be found nowhere else, including intimate contact with the soil, animals, plants, and the weather.

In many states, especially outside the populous East Coast, the state universities (among them some of those described in Chapter 2) are larger and more prestigious, with academic standards as high as those at most private universities. Any of the specialists named above whose titles include the words "agricultural," "animal," or "rural" almost certainly would have attended a state university college of agriculture, for graduate work if not undergraduate. But a holder of a bachelor's degree from any college or university can enter almost any of these professions. A master's degree is always desirable, and to teach at the college level, a doctorate is needed.

Where Would You Work as an Agricultural Scientist?

The agricultural scientist might find employment literally anywhere, from Park Avenue in New York to a village in the Philippines. Major employers include the U.S. Department of Agriculture, state departments of agriculture and natural resources, colleges and universities and their state experiment stations, agribusiness, international agencies, engineering and consulting firms operating around the world, United Nations agencies, and foreign governments with their equivalents of any of the above.

The economics of some areas of technology make them feasible in developing countries but not in the developed nations. The desalinization of saline water, for example, has—not yet—proven economical in the United States. But in Saudi Arabia, which has far more oil than water, an extraordinarily expensive desalting program now meets most of the country's domestic water needs. Giant desalinization plants on the Red Sea process 500 billion gallons a day of water, which is then piped to major cities and agricultural areas hundreds of miles away. Plans are being made to serve every city in Saudi Arabia, and experiments are under way with solar processing systems.

What Do Agricultural Scientists Earn?

According to the College Placement Council, beginning salary offers for agricultural scientists with the bachelor's degree averaged $20,220 a year in 1988.

In the federal government in 1989, agricultural scientists, with the bachelor's and no prior significant experience, could command from $16,875 to $17,438, depending in part on their college records.

Many of these jobs are at agricultural experiment stations affiliated with state land grant colleges and universities. The opportunity usually is afforded to take graduate work, sometimes at reduced tuition.

With an advanced degree, one can advance, at mid-career, to, say, the GS-13 level, paying $44,092 to start.

What Is the Job Future for Agricultural Scientists?

The Bureau of Labor Statistics estimates employment of agricultural scientists at twenty-five thousand, and projects a 21 percent rise, of 5,200, by the year 2000.

The strength of the agricultural sciences will continue to be influenced by three factors:

1. Agriculture traditionally has had a strong rural constituency expressed through farm families and their votes, their congressional representatives, the Department of Agriculture, and the powerful lobbies of agribusiness enterprises.
2. Farmers, the traditional products of agricultural colleges, are being joined in their alumni groups by large numbers of science graduates who have no intention of becoming farmers, and the

"farm bloc" and the broader environmental community together have greatly multiplied political power.

3. There is a third group of citizens with a natural affinity to, and interest in, both agriculture and environment—and that is women. Women comprise about one-third of the total enrollment in agricultural colleges, studying everything from agricultural engineering to zoology.

FISHERIES CONSERVATION

Millions of people who live along the shores of the earth's oceans, seas, bays, lakes, rivers, and streams depend on fish for food, perhaps as their only source of life-supporting protein. In the United States alone, in 1988, commercial fishers harvested five million metric tons of finfish and shellfish products worth $4 billion. Aquaculture (fish farming) of fishes and invertebrates in ponds and other closed systems has grown rapidly in the last two decades. Aquacultural production in North America is roughly 360,000 metric tons—mostly catfish, crawfish, trout, and salmon—valued at $600 million.

Aquaculture is a fascinating career, according to the American Fisheries Society (AFS). So is the management of recreational fisheries. Next to swimming, sport fishing is the most popular outdoor activity in North America. In 1985 U.S. anglers numbered 59 million, or nearly 27 percent of the population. Anglers fished a total of 988 million days and spent over $28 billion on licenses, tackle, food, lodging, boats, motors, transportation, and fuel.

Yet, adds the AFS:

> Our fisheries resources need help. The demands and stresses that have been placed on many fisheries continue to threaten their productivity. Dredging, dam building, and shoreline erosion physically alter aquatic habitats and can kill fish and invertebrates or interfere with reproduction. Withdrawal of water from lakes and streams for domestic, industrial, and agricultural purposes also reduces available habitat. Release of pollutants into the water threatens survival of all aquatic organisms. Overfishing also threatens many fisheries, and competition for various

species of fish by sport, commercial, and subsistence fishermen often leads to conflicts and complicates management.

What Do Fisheries Conservationists Do?

The professional directly concerned with sports and commercial fisheries is the *fisheries conservationist* or *wildlife biologist* specializing in this area. This specialist studies the life history, habits, classifications, and economic relations of aquatic organisms. The science is an applied field, characterized by practical applications of biological sciences, especially managing fish hatcheries, conducting information and education programs for those in sports and commercial fishing, inspecting and grading fishery products for human and animal consumption, and measuring and promoting the market for fresh fish and processed fisheries products.

What Education Would You Need to Become a Fisheries Conservationist?

As in biology and ecology, fisheries conservation occupations require a good high school education, including physics, chemistry, biology, English, communications, mathematics, and a foreign language. Some community colleges offer the associate's degree in fisheries. You can get good preparation at almost any four-year college or university by taking a degree in biology or zoology. Study, for starters, the principles of comparative anatomy, microbiology, genetics, chemistry, mathematics, computer programming, and statistics. Continue to hone your skills in communications, English, and the humanities.

If you prefer a specialized curriculum, seek out one of the 167 colleges or universities offering specialized programs in fisheries science or conservation—including fifteen in Canada and one in Mexico. Many institutions offer an M.S. as well as a B.S. program. If you plan to teach and do research, a Ph.D. is mandatory.

Where Would You Work as a Fisheries Conservationist?

A majority of fisheries conservationists work for the federal, state, provincial, and territorial government agencies of the United States and Canada. Seven agencies of the U.S. Department of the Interior, notably the Fish and Wildlife Service, constitute the largest employer of fisheries conservationists. The National Oceanic and Atmospheric Administration of the Department of Commerce, the Environmental Protection Agency, and components of the Department of Agriculture also employ considerable numbers. Among other significant employers are about two dozen cooperative fishery units such as hatcheries attached to agricultural experiment stations. A few international agencies, such as the Food and Agriculture Organization (FAO) of the United Nations, hire fisheries scientists. Others are employed by private industries to develop food products, compile data, prepare environmental impact statements, or manage aquatic properties. A few are hired by environmental consulting firms, forest product companies, private clubs and organizations to do a variety of work from stream management to public relations.

What Do Fisheries Conservationists Earn?

As civil service salaries for federal employees are standardized, fisheries conservationists in the Department of Agriculture and the Interior are about on a par with agricultural scientists. Hence, the salary range for beginners with no prior significant experience is up to $16,875 per year.

The other information given earlier regarding agricultural scientists would apply, as well, to fisheries scientists.

What Is the Job Future for Fisheries Conservationists?

The American Fisheries Society's current "Careers in Fisheries" folder reports:

> The number of available fisheries positions has expanded in recent years as a result of increased funding under the Federal Aid in Sport Fish

Restoration Act, which distributes funds collected from a federal tax on fishing tackle and other items to the states for fisheries management programs. The increasing demand for fish in our diets has improved the employment picture for students trained in aquaculture. Graduates with strong educational backgrounds and experience in aquaculture and fisheries research and management are always in demand.

While the current *Occupational Outlook Handbook* does not distinguish fisheries conservationists from other conservationists in its estimates, it would appear that there are more than sixteen thousand such specialists. Unless there are favorable changes in national priorities, growth can be expected to be modest, perhaps 15 percent, over the next decade, bringing employment to about 18,500 by the year 2000.

FORESTRY

"What are forests?" asks an expert panel in a new report of the National Research Council (NRC),[1] which provides this definition:

Forests and related renewable natural resources include the organisms, soil, water, and air associated with timberlands as well as forest-related rangelands, grasslands, brushlands, wetlands and swamps, alpine lands and tundra, deserts, wildlife habitat, and watersheds. These resources include many different categories of land ownership: national forests, parks, and grasslands; federal, state, and private wildlife and wilderness areas; national, state, county, municipal, and community parks and forests; private nonindustrial timber and range lands; and industrial forests and rangelands.

Forests and their resources are for people to use. Americans used more than eighty cubic feet of wood products per person in 1989, up from sixty cubic feet only twenty years earlier. Worldwide, demand for wood products has nearly doubled in the past three decades. The U.S. Forest Service predicts demand will increase by another 45 percent by

---

[1]*Forestry Research,* © 1990 by the National Academy of Sciences, National Academy Press, Washington, D.C.

the year 2000. Most important for the future, trees also are regarded as the front line of defense against global warming because of their ability to remove huge amounts of carbon dioxide from the atmosphere and "fix" it at the earth's surface.

Most surprising and disturbing is how much more scientists need to learn about trees and forests, according to the National Research Council report. Research on this vital resource is surprisingly weak and fragmented, it says. Without a substantial infusion of new funds and far more researchers, scientific understanding of forests will be inadequate even to sustain the benefits Americans currently enjoy from them, let alone to meet the needs of a more populous and competitive future.

At the precise time that people expect more from forests and forest research, efforts to learn more actually are being reduced, according to the study committee that wrote the report. Since 1978, the number of undergraduate degrees awarded in forestry and related fields has declined by half. Because of inflation, the static government research budget supports less and less research, while industry's forestry research budget also has decreased. The Forest Service budget for research actually has dropped in buying power by 124 percent over the last decade. Moreover, because of inadequate funding, fewer than 9 percent of grant applications to the forestry competitive grants programs are approved. And many research facilities are outmoded. Says panel chair Dr. John C. Gordon, dean and professor of the School of Forestry and Environmental Studies at Yale University:

> Romantic visions of the forest primeval are fine for storybooks but inadequate for the environmental and economic challenges we face. Without our urban and rural forests, our cities will be hotter, our countryside windier and drier, and our supply of wild birds and animals smaller and less diverse. We need our forests and must learn more about them if we are to keep and use them.

The report calls for the establishment of a new forestry model, an "environmental" approach to forestry problems. This approach "holds that human beings and nature are interrelated, that humans are not superior to the natural world, but depend on the biosphere for their existence." While lumber production will continue, it must be balanced with other needs and done in such a way as to minimize damage to forest ecosystems.

Where to begin? Dr. Gordon suggests, in his preface, that

> . . . the relationships between forestry and agriculture in this country (and elsewhere) need to be enhanced and improved. We believe that the time has come to examine both fields and establish a new sense of partnership between agriculture and forestry. This partnership must be based on a broad understanding of both fields and their essential similarities and differences. It will also require a new vision and renewed vigor in the research that supports both.

In the first half of the twentieth century, many of the leaders of the conservation movement were professional foresters, and many of them were researchers, noted the panel. Today, few public opinion leaders who help shape policy on natural resources are foresters. And unfortunately, "While foresters are accused of having sold out to commercial interests, others (often from narrow special-interest groups) are leading in the reshaping of the conservation movement and of forest-related policy."

What Do Foresters Do?

Just as the NRC panel defined forests, it also defined forestry, as follows:

> Forestry consists of the principles and practices utilized in the management, use, and enjoyment of forests. Forestry includes a broad range of activities—managing timber, fish, wildlife, range, and watershed; protecting forests and timber products from diseases, insects, and fire; harvesting, transporting, manufacturing, marketing, preserving, and protecting wood and other forest products; maintaining water and air quality; and maintaining society's well-being as it is influenced by forests and other renewable natural resources and their derived products and values.

The Society of American Foresters' career information sheet is more down to earth in its list of functions of foresters:

> They direct land surveys, road construction, and the planting and harvesting of trees, applying the economics of forestry. They are skilled

in preventing damage to forest resources from insects, diseases, and fires. They plan and prescribe forestland uses and practices, and work with the people involved. For example, they plan and supervise recreational uses of forestland, timber harvesting crews, fire fighters, and tree planters. Foresters administer forest properties, government agencies, and forest companies. Others research or teach in the field of forestry. Foresters work with the general public and forest owners in making America's forests a world model of health, beauty, and productivity.

What Education Would You Need to Become a Forester?

The professional forester must have at least a bachelor's degree in forestry from one of the approximately fifty schools of forestry. If possible, you should consider the M.S. or Ph.D., especially if you intend to concentrate on teaching and research. The curriculum includes a well-rounded education in the biological, physical, and social sciences. Specialized studies include concentrations in ecology, forest economics, forest protection, silviculture, resources management and use, dendrology, forest measurements, forest policy, and forest administration. Forestry schools usually require the student to spend one summer in a college-operated field camp and encourage spending other summers in related work, if possible.

Where Would You Work as a Forester?

An estimated 50 percent of professional foresters work for public agencies—federal, state, and local. Some 32 percent are employed by industrial concerns, mainly pulp and paper, lumber, logging, and milling companies. The remaining 18 percent work in the forestry industry, teach, do research, or are in graduate school.

The principal employing organization is the U.S. Forest Service of the Department of Agriculture. The Soil Conservation Service also is a major employer. Many foresters also work in components of the Department of the Interior: Bureau of Land Management, U.S. Fish and Wildlife Service, and National Park Service. A forester employed by a state would work in the comparable state agency.

What Do Foresters Earn?

The same pay scales given earlier for agricultural scientists and fisheries conservationists apply, in general, to foresters as well.

In recent newsletters, jobs were offered in those salary ranges throughout the nation. A university in Minnesota in 1990 paid $45,000 for a research associate in tree improvement. Jobs available in all sections of the United States pay hourly wages of $10–$15.

What Is the Job Future for Foresters?

There are an estimated 27,000 professional foresters in the United States. Due to budgetary constraints, a modest 8 percent rise, to a level of 29,300, is predicted by the year 2000.

In recent years the number of degrees in forestry has exceeded occupational requirements, creating competition for jobs. If the number of degrees granted each year remains at present levels, competition is expected to persist. Opportunities will be better for those who can offer an employer either an advanced degree or several years' experience.

If the forestry profession and the forest products industries, with their friends in Congress, were able to take advantage of the ammunition provided in the *Mandate for Change* report, the employment picture could change. That they have not to date is rather surprising. Newspapers and magazines are printed on paper, and many publishing giants own their own paper mills. Television finds nature programs attract viewers, and forest-products companies sponsor a great deal of public television programming. The media giants have many reasons to support forestry research.

RANGE MANAGEMENT

You have seen it in Western movies on TV: It is native grazing land, called rangelands. It covers about 47 percent of the entire land area of the earth. It is the largest single category of land in the U.S.—more than one billion acres, mostly in the western states and Alaska.

Rangelands contain many natural resources: grass and shrubs for animal grazing, habitats for livestock and wildlife, facilities for water sports and other kinds of recreation, and areas for scientific study of the environment. These renewable resources can yield their full potential only if properly managed.

What Do Range Managers Do?

The *range manager*—sometimes called *range conservationisi, range scientist* or *range ecologist*—manages, improves, and protects this ecological system. Become a range manager and you would be responsible for deciding the number and kind of animals to be grazed. You would be a practical ecologist, selecting the best season for grazing while conserving soil and vegetation for other uses, such as wildlife grazing, outdoor recreation, watersheds, and growing timber. You would be a practical economist, optimizing the production of livestock and sometimes timber and commercial crops.

You would restore or improve rangelands through techniques such as controlled burning, reseeding, and the biological, chemical or mechanical control of undesirable plants. You would have the satisfaction of seeing your surroundings change as a result of your work. You might plow up rangelands covered by natural sagebrush vegetation and reseed them with more productive grass.

Because of the multiple use of rangelands, you might spend much of your working time performing the duties of a forester, wildlife conservationist, watershed manager, recreationist, or even a farmer! You might have to provide animal watering facilities, control erosion, and build pens and fences, for example.

What Education Would You Need to Become a Range Manager?

A bachelor's degree in range management is the normal educational qualification for a professional position in the field. A degree in a closely related field such as agronomy or forestry, including courses in range management, may be accepted. Approximately twenty colleges and universities offer degrees in range management; all of them offer the master's degree; some schools offer a Ph.D. in range science or a related field.

A degree in range management requires a basic knowledge of biology, chemistry, physics, mathematics, and communications skills. Advanced courses combine plant, animal, and soil sciences with principles of ecology and resources management. Desirable electives include economics, computer science, forestry, wildlife, and recreation.

Where Would You Work as a Range Manager?

The majority of range managers work for federal, state, and local governments, almost exclusively in the western half of the U.S. or Canada. Federal employees work mainly in the Forest Service and Soil Conservation Service of the Department of Agriculture and in the Bureau of Land Management of the Department of the Interior. State and provincial game and fish departments employ many range managers.

In the private sector, livestock ranches are the largest employers. Some range managers work as rangeland appraisers for banks and real estate firms. Others manage their own lands. A few teach and do research at colleges and universities or work overseas with U.S. or United Nations agencies.

What Do Range Managers Earn?

Information given previously in this chapter for other conservation professionals applies to range managers as well.

The Bureau of Land Management regularly advertises for range managers at the GS-5 to GS-7 levels, depending upon education and experience. The starting salary range is $16,875 to $25,569.

What Is the Job Future for Range Managers?

Employment opportunities for range managers are expected to grow faster than the average for all occupations, through the year 2000. The growing demands for red meat, wildlife habitat, recreation, and water, as well as increasing environmental concerns, should stimulate the need for more range managers, Since the amount of land cannot be expanded, range managers will need to increase the range ecosystem's productivity while maintaining its environmental quality. Also, range managers will be in greater demand to manage large ranches, which are increasing in number. Some of these "spreads" in the western United States are being acquired by super-rich Middle Eastern oil potentates as investments in a country which they consider safe, prosperous, and inviting. Wealthy Americans, as well, are buying ranches for sport, vacation, and investments.

As oil and coal exploration accelerates, private industry will require many more range specialists to reclaim or restore mine lands to productivity, as required by federal law.

SOIL CONSERVATION

Back in the 1930s, the United States lost millions of acres of fertile, productive soil in the Great Plains states due to drought and wind erosion. Deforestation of vast areas of Africa, Asia, and South America are subjecting the ecology, the resources, and the people to traumatic losses, possibly changing the climates of continents. In most cases, those are crass, *preventable* losses—and they persist today, on a smaller scale, in this country.

What Do Soil Conservationists Do?

As a *soil conservationist* you would be responsible for supplying farmers, ranchers, and others with technical assistance. Such landowners are organized under state law into soil conservation districts. While these people would be your "clients," the chances are that you would work for the federal government in helping them to adjust land use, protect land against soil deterioration, rebuild eroded and depleted soils, and stabilize runoff and sediment-producing areas. You also would help improve cover on lands devoted to raising crops and maintaining forests, pasture, and rangelands and the wildlife they support. In addition, you probably would help plan methods and facilities for handling water for farm and ranch use, conserving water, reducing damage from flood water and sediment, and draining or irrigating farms or ranches as needed.

As a soil conservationist (or soil scientist or soil engineer) you would draw maps portraying soil, water, vegetation, and structures. You would compile information including cost-benefit analyses (the costs of various uses and treatment of lands and the relative benefits to be expected). You would present these maps and plans to the landowner or operator and answer any questions. When the operator had decided on a plan of action for conservation farming or ranching, you would provide any needed counsel and technical advice and guidance on implementation of the plan.

You might work on a special program of the Soil Conservation Service (SCS), such as snow surveys and water forecasting. Each winter SCS personnel cover about 70,000 miles of the western states by skis, oversnow vehicles, and aircraft to measure the snowpack. The data they collect are translated into a water supply forecast for the following spring and summer planting and growing seasons.

New federal antipollution laws impose strict controls on sediment, or soil runoff, responsible for much water pollution. So, many states employ soil scientists to inspect large highway and building sites where vegetation has been removed and agricultural lands where fertilizers have been applied, to make sure proper erosion control methods have been used.

What Education Would You Need
to Become a Soil Conservationist?

As a minimum you should have a bachelor of science degree with a major in soil conservation or a closely related area of natural science or agriculture. Courses in chemistry, physics, mathematics, topography, meteorology, agronomy, and related physical and environmental sciences are desirable. As you would be responsible for communicating and interpreting plans and counseling users on their problems, you should take as many liberal arts courses as your college program permits. These should include English, psychology, speech, and possibly education.

If you were raised on a farm or ranch, you would have an advantage over others in a "feel" for landowners' needs. If you came from the city or suburbs, on the other hand, you would need to compensate for a probable deficiency in "feel" by trying to get summer jobs in rural settings—if necessary, working for room and board to get the experience.

Where Would You Work as a Soil Conservationist?

Most soil conservationists work for the federal government, mainly the U.S. Department of Agriculture's Soil Conservation Service. Other federal employers are the Forest Service, National Park Service, and Bureau of Reclamation. Private employment is increasing. Banks, public utilities, real estate developers, and consulting engineers also employ soil conservationists.

What Do Soil Conservationists Earn?

The information given previously for agricultural scientists and foresters generally applies to soil conservationists, too.

What Is the Job Future for Soil Conservationists?

The rapid expansion of water supply, waste water, and other urban environmental programs has accelerated openings for soil conservationists in urban areas, as has industrial development including the conversion of rural land to industrial parks. Growing demand for new energy sources, for expanding food production, for new housing and new communities—all these factors—will require more soil conservationists and related personnel.

There are an estimated twenty thousand soil conservationists and scientists in the United States. Despite the need for more, funding constraints will hold growth to about 5 percent, or about one thousand more positions by the year 2000.

WILDLIFE MANAGEMENT

More than 130 million persons in the United States and Canada, and millions more on all continents, enjoy hunting, viewing, and/or feeding wildlife, according to a survey reported by The Wildlife Society, the organization for professionals. Commercial trapping (and its counterpart, commercial fishing) produce protein nutrition for millions. Farmers and others who hunt feed their families, in part, from what they shoot and bag.

Wild animals are part of the natural heritage of the American and other peoples. Species may need protection when they become scarce. Scarcity or extinction almost always is the result of vital habitats being destroyed or altered by deliberate environmental development. Destruction, sometimes wanton, occurs when people destroy animals such as rabbits, blackbirds, deer and others that forage on crops, rangelands or gardens, destroying plants being grown for use.

Wildlife is defined as all animals that are not domesticated. In practical terms, it generally means *game* species that are harvested for food, sport or other reasons. Game animals are controlled or managed by the manipulation of habitat and by the establishment of seasons, licenses, and bag limits.

What Do Wildlife Managers Do?

Several natural resources professions have moved away from using the word *conservation* in job titles because of its connotations of *protection* or *preservation* rather than beneficial *use* and *regeneration*. (Example: range management.)

The Wildlife Society defines *wildlife management* as:

. . . human effort to maintain or manipulate natural resources, including soil, water, plants, and animals (including man) for the best interests of the environment (including man) whether these interests be ecological, commercial, recreational or scientific.

A wildlife manager has a professional goal to assure continued, satisfactory population levels of wildlife. One important job of the wildlife manager is to gather data through research to formulate and to apply scientifically sound solutions to wildlife species or habitat problems. Another job is to conduct on-the-ground management programs, enforce regulations, administer programs or properties. An equally important effort is to inform others about wildlife, its ecology and its management.

What Education Would You Need to Become a Wildlife Manager?

You can take suitable bachelor's level work, say, in biology, at almost any college or university, and this would be sufficient for a beginning job in wildlife biology. In addition to a thorough grounding in physical and biological sciences, you would need training in such liberal arts as English, languages, history, geography, statistics, and the economics of food and fiber production. While still in high school, you should take as many mathematics, physics, English, chemistry, and biology courses as you can. The Wildlife Society recommends that you acquire group experience in committee work and meetings and write for high school publications, as well.

If you know upon graduating from high school that wildlife conservation or management is the field for you, you might choose one of the almost one hundred colleges and universities listed by The Wildlife Society in its annual survey of enrollments.

The minimum educational requirements for certification are a four-year course of study in an accredited college or university, leading to a bachelor's or higher degree in wildlife. Among the courses required are the biological sciences; wildlife management; ecology and botany; physical sciences; mathematics through calculus; computer science; humanities, social sciences, and English composition; and environmental policy, administration, law, law enforcement, land-use planning, and other electives.

Where Would You Work as a Wildlife Manager?

Most wildlife conservationists in the U.S. and Canada work for the federal government, state, or provincial governments or in colleges and universities. Many of these programs are cooperative, that is, funded largely by the U.S. Government but conducted in state facilities by state employees.

In a 1982 survey, The Wildlife Society found that federal agencies hired the most bachelor's degree graduates, state agencies the most master's degree recipients, and colleges and universities the most doctorate holders. Only university hiring increased over a two-year period.

The federal sector remained the largest employer, hiring 34 percent of those graduates obtaining wildlife employment. Within the federal government, the U.S. Forest Service was the largest overall employer, with 25 percent; it also hired the most bachelor's degree graduates, with the U.S. Fish and Wildlife Service second by both measures.

What Do Wildlife Managers Earn?

The compensation picture for wildlife managers is similar to that of other conservationists covered above.

What Is the Job Future for Wildlife Managers?

There are about twenty thousand wildlife managers and conservationists in the United States. A modest 5 percent growth, to twenty-one thousand, is expected by the year 2000.

Growth of the wildlife field could be accelerated if some body, such as the National Research Council or the Department of the Interior, were to undertake a study equivalent to *Opportunities in Biology* or *Fisheries Research,* described earlier. Such fact-finding studies often have led to significant revitalization of other fields—for example, environmental protection in the 1970s and 1980s.

WHERE SHOULD YOU WRITE FOR MORE INFORMATION?

American Fisheries Society
5410 Grosvenor Lane
Bethesda, Md. 20814-2199

American Society of Agricultural Engineers
2950 Niles Road
St. Joseph, Mich. 49085

American Water Resources Association
5410 Grosvenor Lane
Bethesda, Md. 20814

National Wildlife Federation
1400 Sixteenth Street, N.W.
Washington, D.C. 20036-2266

Society for Range Management
1839 York Street
Denver, Colo. 80206

Society of American Foresters
5400 Grosvenor Lane
Bethesda, Md. 20814

Soil Conservation Society of America
7515 N.W. Ankeny Road
Ankeny, Iowa 50021

The Wildlife Society
5410 Grosvenor Lane
Bethesda, Md. 20814

CHAPTER 6

LAND USE AND HUMAN SETTLEMENTS

Misuse of the land is now one of the most serious and difficult challenges to environmental quality, because it is the most out-of-hand, and irreversible. Land use is still not guided by any agreed upon standards. It is instead influenced by a welter of sometimes competing, overlapping government institutions and programs, private and public attitudes and biases, and distorted economic incentives.—*First Annual Report on Environmental Quality,* 1970.

PROFESSIONS COVERED

Architecture, Geography, Landscape Architecture, Urban and Regional Planning

Social decisions about land use involve the very fabric of society. Individuals and families, in constant change and frequent moves, create impacts on the land of which they are scarcely aware. So do governmental decisions about development, housing, transportation, agriculture, water resources, and the like. So do private industry's various moves— to build a factory, shopping center, power plant, and so forth. Conflicts of many kinds are inevitable in such drastic social change as land use control. Private property vs. public environmental concerns is perhaps the foremost conflict. Economic growth, payrolls, and jobs vs. open land and low-density population is another. And environmental protection vs. energy needs is a third.

So we have conflicting feelings about the land. As we saw in the preceding chapter, we want to preserve much of it for our own and future generations' use and enjoyment. At the same time, we want to be free—and others to be free—to own and use as much of it as we can afford. Yet, there is a finite amount of land. And the population of the United States still grows by one to two million per year. What kind of environment our children and their children inhabit is being determined today, to some degree, by such public policies as public housing subsidies, mortgage guarantees, and federal tax provisions favoring home ownership.

Land use traditionally has been, and remains, primarily a local responsibility. What one is allowed to do with one's private property is determined by local laws and regulations, established and enforced by local government. Architects, landscape architects, and planners, three of the professionals discussed here, generally work on a project at a time, and it is the local jurisdiction that controls their work there.

TRENDS IN LAND USE

The Council on Environmental Quality has been observing major national trends in land use since its inception in 1970. These include the continuing loss of agricultural lands to urbanization; desertification, the spread of desert-like conditions to areas that once were more productive; population changes, both large geographic shifts westward and southward and suburbanization around cities; and the special problems of the coastal zone and impact of encroachment on wetlands and marine resources.

Environmentalists recognized early in the new environmental era that the new tools of social and economic analysis would permit assessing the costs versus the benefits of federal actions affecting the environment. They searched for an "action-forcing" mechanism to assure that the federal government could follow through on any pledges to protect the environment.

The device found and made the keystone of the National Environmental Policy Act (NEPA) of 1969 is its section 102(2)(c). This section requires each federal agency to prepare an environmental impact statement in advance of every major action, recommendation, or report on legislation that may significantly affect the quality of the human environment. Hundreds of different types of activities are covered, and thousands of cases have been filed under NEPA since it was implemented in 1970. The Council on Environmental Quality reports for 1988, the latest figures available, that ninety-one cases were filed by federal agencies, and 100 other complaints were filed by environmental groups, individuals, state or local governments, business groups, and Indian tribes.

Environmental impact statements (not cases) filed by federal agencies numbered 430 in 1988, and 370 in 1989. Virtually all involved land use, in such forms as road construction, land acquisition, mining, forestry and range management, water supply, wetlands, military installations, sewage treatment plants, power facilities, solid waste, housing subdivisions and new communities, and many more.

The Council on Environmental Quality is a reliable source of environmental data and trends analysis. In its Twentieth Annual Report, the council shows that the total land, in millions of acres, increased sharply in 1959 with the addition of Alaska and Hawaii as states. But that did not change the virtually steady increase, since the turn of the century, in cropland. However, forest land has steadily decreased since 1959. Despite the continuing rapid urbanization of the United States, total acreage devoted to agricultural use has not declined since 1959.

ARCHITECTURE

Architecture is the art and science of design, according to the careers brochure of The American Institute of Architects, which elaborates:

Architects are professionals who organize space in, around, and among buildings to satisfy man's need for shelter. They must be artists, engineers, social scientists, and environmentalists in their search for creative solutions to design problems that respond to function—how the building "works" for its users; structure—how it will be constructed; form—how effects of volume, shape, color, and texture interact to express the esthetic quality of the whole; economy—how to balance the project requirements within the client's budget; environment—how the building "fits" in its natural and climatic setting; and regulation—how the building protects the safety, comfort, and well-being of its occupants.

Such a broad functional statement barely suggests the range of the architect's work. This work also involves the redesign of existing facilities and the design of new facilities. It ranges in scale from the design of an individual space to the development of comprehensive urban, regional, even national plans.

What Do Architects Do?

Architects may be engaged in private practice or work for architectural, engineering, and planning firms; for government agencies; commercial, industrial, and institutional organizations such as hotel-motel chains, restaurant operators, or fast-food businesses; and for development and real estate companies.

An individual or firm may choose to specialize in a particular building type: schools, housing, retirement communities, hospitals or nursing homes, even golf courses and other recreation facilities.

Many specialize in such areas as marketing, project management, programming, specifications-writing, energy conservation, or estimating and cost control. Others pursue allied professions such as planning, landscape architecture, interior design, or historic preservation.

Architectural services often begin with programming, the research and analysis of client needs that will form the basis of a design project; schematic design, the preliminary, conceptual stage of a project that fixes its broadest outlines; design development, a "fleshing out" of the scheme with dimensions, materials, and details; construction documents, the preparation of drawings and specifications that fully describe a project for construction; bidding and negotiation, providing assistance to clients in arriving at a contract for construction; and construction administration, overseeing the progress of the work and the payment of contractors.

Architects must meet frequently with clients to determine needs, advise on decisions, report on progress and costs, and review plans. They will consult with other design professionals who may be engaged as members of the project team: structural, mechanical, and electrical engineers, soils and civil engineers; land use planners and landscape architects; construction cost estimators; lighting, acoustical, and energy conservation specialists; and interior designers—all working under the direction and supervision of the architect, who is responsible for the overall coordination of the work.

These are the professionals who also consult with local planning, zoning, and building code officials, and should be knowledgeable of current codes and regulations affecting site planning and construction. They also may be required to coordinate with neighborhood organizations, lending institutions, developers, and real estate interests, and must be able to work closely with contractors and materials and equipment manufacturers and suppliers.

Architectural firms must expend great effort to market their services to potential clients to ensure a steady and growing workload of projects in the office. This means photography and graphic arts are important professional tools, and firms must produce brochures and proposals that include drawings, photos, and written descriptions of previous work. Most offices maintain a large library of slides and renderings for presentation purposes.

The architect frequently employs, or works with as consultants, the other disciplines covered in this chapter, and even more: builders, land-use lawyers, codes officials, and *architectural historians*. In recent years, architectural history has emerged as more than an esoteric subject. Fueled by the historic preservation movement, it has become a significant and growing profession in the United States, Canada, Great Britain, and most mainland European countries. The bachelor or master of architectural history is qualification for a professional job in government or the private sector. Every state has an office with historic-preservation responsibilities; one of the federal-state programs administered through that office provides tax credits to citizens, including developers, who restore qualifying properties for renewal and reuse.

What Education Would You Need to Become an Architect?

All fifty states and the District of Columbia require architects to be licensed to practice. Candidates must successfully complete a rigorous, four-day examination. Among the areas covered are site and building design, predesign, building systems, structural technology; mechanical, plumbing, electrical, and life safety systems; materials and methods; and construction documents and services. In most states, the first professional degree in architecture must be from one of the ninety-four accredited schools of architecture. Graduate education beyond the first professional degree may be desirable for research, teaching, and certain specialties.

Graduates of first-professional-degree programs generally must serve an internship under the supervision of a licensed architect before being admitted to the architecture registration examination. Three years of apprenticeship is required in most states.

Where Would You Work as an Architect?

As a new graduate, you usually would begin as a junior draftsperson in an architectural firm. Under supervision, you would make drawings and models of structures. You could advance, after several years, to chief or senior draftsperson responsible for all major details of a set of working drawings, and possibly directing the work of others. If you are outstanding, and if the partners of the firm have an opening, they might make you an associate. Then you would receive, in addition to a salary, a share of the profits. You might, of course, leave your employer and join with others to form your own architectural firm or establish a private practice alone.

Most architects work for architectural firms or for contractors, real estate and development firms or other businesses that have large construction programs. Only a small percentage work for the federal government, primarily for the Departments of Defense, the Interior, Housing and Urban Development, and the General Services Administration.

What Do Architects Earn?

According to the American Institute of Architects, graduates of professional degree programs working as intern-architects earn around $20,000 a year. Beginning salaries depend upon the size, type, and geographical location of the employing organization.

Those with managerial responsibilities in large architectural firms may have salaries and bonuses exceeding $100,000 a year. The earnings of self-employed architects vary considerably and depend upon the size, nature, and specialization of their offices, the scope of professional services offered, and geographic location.

In 1988, the average salary for architects in the federal government was about $39,500.

What Is the Job Future for Architects?

The architectural function is essential to many types of enterprises. Companies as diverse as developers of office buildings and shopping malls, and operators of fast-food chains, hotels/motels, recreation and resort operations, hospitals and nursing homes, all employ architectural staff or contract architects.

All those industries, as well as home building, are vulnerable to economic depression, inflation, and war. In the 1980s, when the price of oil fell due to a glut in supply and falling prices, the economies of Houston, Dallas, and other Sun Belt cities were hard hit, and many skyscrapers and malls remained closed and empty. Concurrently, the savings and loan scandals hit hardest at the building industry. When Iraq's aggression in 1990 called for the United Nations' military buildup in the Persian Gulf, culminating in Operation Desert Storm, the domestic economy was further upset, as always happens in war. The demand for architects is highly dependent upon the local level of construction, residential and nonresidential, as well as upon national economic conditions.

There are about ninety thousand architecture graduates in the United States, with considerable unemployment in 1991. Writing in 1988, the BLS was very optimistic, forecasting a 25 percent growth by the turn of the century—the addition of twenty-two thousand new or replacement openings. Such optimism, at this writing, seems misplaced.

Then there are the significant but logical career changes: from architecture into graphic design, advertising, visual arts, product design, construction contracting and supervision, real estate or investments. One could get a job with government or with a consulting firm, perhaps preparing environmental impact studies and statements. Teaching, journalism, architecture criticism, photography—all are ancillary areas into which architects can move.

Finally, there always is the possibility of a drastic career change such as joining the Peace Corps or a private philanthropy, say Habitat for Humanity, a nonprofit organization which is building or rehabilitating affordable housing in Appalachia, in New York City, and in the developing nations of Africa and elsewhere.

GEOGRAPHY

The Association of American Geographers, in a careers publication, calls *geography* "an especially attractive major for Liberal Arts students." Geography provides a foundation for a number of possible occupations, and a regional and world perspective required of responsible citizens, according to the publication's authors, professors at Dartmouth College, who define the discipline as follows:

> Geography is the study of place, or space, in the same sense that history is the study of time. The geographer's method of inquiry concentrates on asking two essential questions: "WHERE are things located?" and "WHY are they located where they are?" While the answer to the former is largely descriptive, the answer to the latter is entirely analytical. The geographer is concerned primarily with interpreting and explaining the occurrence, distribution, and interrelationships of the physical and cultural elements which can be discerned in the landscape.

What Do Geographers Do?

As a *geographer,* you might use advanced statistical techniques, mathematical models, maps, and a computer. In the field, you might interview people, inspect terrain and features of the "built" environment, and take precise measurements with surveying and meteorological instruments. As a member of a research team, you would have available data and observations made by others: maps, aerial photographs, and data compiled by remote sensing instruments on earth satellites and returned to earth by telecommunications facilities.

The Association of American Geographers emphasizes how practical geography is and cites the geographic studies which first showed how widespread is contamination by radon. Radon is an invisible, odorless radioactive gas produced by the decay of uranium in rock and soil. In 1988, the National Research Council released a report in which it was estimated that radon is responsible for five thousand to twenty thousand lung cancer deaths per year in the United States. As a result, the Environmental Protection Agency inaugurated a program in areas of highest incidence to shield children in schools, and the public in federal buildings, from radon emissions. This was followed by a nationwide public information program to alert parents, in particular, to the hazards of overexposure of children to radon gas. Test kits for the consumer are quite inexpensive, but if a residence is found to have a high radon level, correcting it may be expensive, on the order of $10,000 for an average residence.

Most geographers specialize. *Economic geographers* focus on the geographic distribution of economic activities. *Political geographers, urban geographers,* and *regional geographers* help define political boundaries and plan governmental activities. *Physical geographers* study the impacts of the earth's configuration on human and environmental activities. *Cartographers* compile and interpret data and design and construct maps and charts. *Medical geographers* study the effects of the environment on human health, working with environmental health officials, biostatisticians, and others to project disease trends and to plan epidemiological control methods and health care facilities. Those major specialties within geography can be broken down further into many subfields.

In 1985 the National Geographic Society, publisher of the *National Geographic* magazine, launched a long-term, nationwide campaign to improve the quality of geography instruction in elementary and secondary schools. The society had ample evidence, from studies and polls, that young Americans were geographically illiterate. Many could not look at a world map and find the Persian Gulf, Vietnam, or the Soviet Union. Many misnamed the nation to the immediate south of the United States or could not distinguish Iowa from Idaho on the U.S. map.

In an international survey in 1989, young Soviet adults scored significantly higher than their American counterparts in identifying locations on a world map. The 18- to 24-year-olds in the Soviet Union correctly identified an average of 9.3 out of sixteen locations worldwide. So did young adults surveyed in Canada and Italy, and Swedish students scored even higher. But in the United States, the average, in sixteen tries, was only 6.9 correct answers.

What Education Would You Need to Become a Geographer?

Approximately 375 U.S. and Canadian colleges and universities offer a four-year undergraduate degree with a geography major. Required are a minimum of twenty-four semester hours or thirty-six quarter hours beyond introductory geography courses. Degree requirements vary among colleges, but most require a broad base of coursework which may include physical, human, cultural, economic, regional geography; meteorology and climatology; cartography, map interpretation, and map design; remote sensing and air photo interpretation; geographic information systems; environmental studies or resource management; and tourism or planning.

Although many graduates obtain positions with a bachelor's degree, better-paying, more challenging positions usually require at least a master's degree.

Where Would You Work as a Geographer?

About one-third of professional geographers teach in colleges and universities. The federal government is the second-largest employer, principally in the Departments of Defense, Interior, Commerce, and Agriculture. Other agencies with significant cadres of geographers are the Environmental Protection Agency, Smithsonian Institution, National Aeronautics and Space Administration, and the Central Intelligence Agency. State and local governments employ others, in the agencies comparable to those named above for the federal establishment.

Magazine and book publishers such as the National Geographic Society employ some geographers, as do the publishers who produce maps, including the oil companies' roadmaps, geologists' maps and atlases. Increasingly, consulting engineering and management firms hire geographers.

What Do Geographers Earn?

The U.S. Office of Personnel Management confirms that geographers are hired, when suitable openings are announced, at the starting-level grade of GS-5 with a salary of $16,875. Mid-level positions frequently are at the GS-12/13 levels, with a range of $37,000 to $44,000 to start.

What is the Job Future for Geographers?

In a recent search of jobs newsletters, no jobs were found for geographers per se. However, numerous openings apparently were broad enough for such an education to be qualifying. These were jobs, among others, as analyst, ombudsman, trainer, planner, information and education specialist, teacher, technical publications editor, school or camp director, and environmental educator. They called, generally, for "degrees or experience in environmental sciences or related field."

The Bureau of Labor Statistics sees little or no employment growth in colleges and universities. But it is optimistic about opportunities in urban and environmental management and planning, including location analysis, land and water resources management, and environmental health planning. "Those with strong backgrounds in cartography, remote sensing imagery interpretation, computer mapping, physical geography, and quantitative techniques should be in particular demand,'' says the BLS, adding:

> The Federal Government will need additional personnel to work in programs such as health planning, regional development, environmental quality, and intelligence. Employment of geographers in state and local government is expected to expand, particularly in health planning; conservation; environmental quality; highway planning; and city, community and regional planning and development. Private industry is expected to hire increasing numbers of geographers for market research and location analysis.

LANDSCAPE ARCHITECTURE

At least two factors go into the achievement of an attractive new or restored community, office or factory building, shopping center, airport, college campus, or, for that matter, residence. Foremost is the building or buildings. Second is the setting or surroundings, combined with the landscaping. Even an ordinary brick or glass-wall low-rise office building, warehouse, or factory can be fully appreciated if the trees, shrubbery plantings, flower beds, and lawns are tastefully designed and the design skillfully executed. The professional often contracted with to design these adornments—to ''make it all work together''—is the *landscape architect*.

What Do Landscape Architects Do?

Some nursery companies offer landscaping services, free with purchase of nursery stock or on payment of a fee, to the average individual homeowner. Owners of large estates may employ professional landscape architects to establish initial landscape plans, to maintain the developed landscape, or to make significant changes on the premises. Otherwise, except perhaps in the most affluent communities, such professionals work mainly on public, commercial, or multiunit residential projects.

Landscape architects are employed by real estate development firms starting new industrial-park projects, municipalities constructing airports or public parks, or investors planning hotel, golf course, or similar resort developments. They often are involved in the project from conception, participating with investors, bankers, lawyers, planners, zoning officials, and historic preservationists in assessing the suitability of, and adapting, the property for the intended purpose. The owners-to-be may ask these professionals' advice on the feasibility of spending the necessary investment vs. the expected payoff. A big development project requires complicated teamwork.

Once the project is begun, landscape architects work closely with architects and engineers to help determine the best arrangement of roads and buildings. They create detailed plans indicating new topography; vegetation such as trees or shrubbery to be retained; trees, shrubs, and flower beds to be added; walkways, driveways, parking areas; such recreation amenities as tennis courts and ponds, if any; artificial lighting; and inviting entranceways to facilities. The service entrance must be made accessible but inconspicuous and the refuse collection area shielded from public view.

Often-subtle factors include the natural elements of the site, such as the climate, soil, rock outcroppings, vegetation, slope of the land, and drainage. The designers must consider open spaces and anticipate the patterns cast upon the building by sunlight, clouds, and other images at different seasons. If there is a stream or lake, a historic or an archaeological site, a cemetery or Indian burial ground—all these must be considered for preservation.

If desirable and appropriate, resting places, picnic tables, benches, a garden, or bicycle and bridle trails, would be incorporated early.

After studying and analyzing the site and its amenities, the landscape architect prepares a preliminary design, which must be submitted to the client for approval. Many changes usually must be made before a design is accepted. New techniques of computer-aided design systems (CADS) make the design stages much faster and far more cost effective than ever before.

The landscape architect makes lists of building materials, determines specifications, and invites landscape contractors to bid for the work.

Costs are always a factor in a building project and tend to rise because the prices of components are constantly rising—and because clients change their minds. The landscape architect is responsible, with others on the design team, for preparing careful cost estimates, economizing wherever possible, revising regularly, and keeping the client and team colleagues apprised of any changes. The actual design work, assisted by computer programs, involves sketches, models, written reports, photographs, land-use slides, and never-ending cost changes.

Some landscape architects specialize in a particular type of work, such as residential development, historic landscape restoration, waterfront improvements, parks and playgrounds, shopping centers, or industrial parks. Still others work in regional planning and resource management, urban redevelopment, environmental impact assessment, or energy conservation through plantings—a properly sited or shaded building can be heated or cooled with a minimum of fuel consumption.

What Education Would You Need
to Become A Landscape Architect?

A bachelor's degree in landscape architecture, which takes four or five years, is the minimum educational requirement for entering the profession. About fifty colleges offer programs which are accredited by the American Society of Landscape Architects.

Most schools advise the high school student to take courses in art, botany, and more mathematics than the minimum required for college entrance. Some also require a high school course in mechanical or geometrical drawing. Otherwise, the requirements for admission are similar to those for architecture, engineering, or science. College technical courses would include surveying, landscape and architectural design, landscape construction, plant materials and design, sketching, recreation and city planning, contracts, specifications, cost estimates, and business practices. You should especially enjoy the field trips, and if you are fortunate, you may get some practical job experience while still in college.

Forty-one states require a license, based on the results of a uniform national licensing examination, for independent practice of landscape architecture.

Where Would You Work as a Landscape Architect?

Virtually all landscape architects are in the private sector, working in their own, usually small, businesses, or for architectural, landscaping, or engineering firms. Others are employed by government agencies concerned with forest management, water storage, public housing, city planning, urban renewal, highways, parks, recreation, or energy conservation. Of the total 20,000 licensed landscape architects, fewer than one thousand work for the federal government, mainly in the Departments of Agriculture, Defense, Energy, and Interior.

What Do Landscape Architects Earn?

Refer to the section on earnings for architects. Even though landscape architecture is a different field, it is practiced in much the same manner, and earnings scales for one parallel and approximate those for the other.

What Is The Job Future For Landscape Architects?

The Bureau of Labor Statistics expects employment of landscape architects to grow faster than the average for all occupations through the year 2000. (A 30 percent growth would provide six thousand new openings.) Nevertheless, economic conditions will continue to affect building projects, and employment expectations—in this or any other field—may or may not be met.

The environmental and energy conservation movements will provide most of the expected thrust. Landscape architects will continue to be in demand for planning and designing attractive suburbs and shopping centers. Local ordinances are tightening up requirements for beautifying office parks, medical clinics, schools, hospitals, and other such developments. Companies are compelled by public relations, if not zoning regulations, to make headquarters, plants, and local offices conform to high standards of landscaping. Utilities use landscaping to camouflage power stations. Legislation requires the participation of landscape architects in hiding unsightly businesses such as junkyards and in planning transportation systems, outdoor recreation areas, and industrial parks. Finally, federal legislation mandates the reclamation of strip-mined lands, the preservation of historic areas and facilities, and coastal zone management—in all of which the landscape architect has a key role.

URBAN AND REGIONAL PLANNING

The term *urban and regional planning* is used here, and by the Bureau of Labor Statistics (BLS) and the American Planning Association (APA), to distinguish this type of planning from social planning or corporate and business planning.

Urban and regional planning, in the definition of the APA, "is a systematic, creative approach used to address and resolve social, physical, and economic problems of neighborhoods, cities, suburbs, metropolitan areas, and larger regions." This planning is focused on the human environment. Its practitioners might be called community or city planners. We choose to call them urban and regional planners.

What Do Urban And Regional Planners Do?

These planners, says the APA,

. . . formulate plans and policies to meet social, economic, and physical needs, and they develop the strategies to make these plans work. Planning is both science and art. It demands technical competence as well as creativity, [and] hardheaded pragmatism and an ability to envision alternatives to the physical and social environments in which we live.

Urban and regional planners, according to the BLS, develop programs to provide for growth and revitalization of urban, suburban, and rural communities and their regions. Planners address such issues as central city redevelopment, traffic congestion, and the impact of growth and change on an area. They formulate capital improvement plans to construct new school buildings, parks and playgrounds, public housing, and water and sewerage systems. They explore locations for sewage treatment and solid-waste disposal facilities, and for chemical, hazardous, and nuclear waste sites. They develop policies and programs for the protection of wetlands, wildlife refuges, archaeological sites, and historic monuments. As the last of the unprotected Civil War battlefields is threatened by development, planners are searching for ways the land can be bought and the landscape preserved.

Inquire about careers of the APA, and you will be sent a packet of materials elaborating on the above description, with a letter which says:

> Planning is a profession in which a diversity of techniques is utilized to bring about positive change. As such, planners must bring a broad perspective to problem-solving efforts affecting a range of social, economic, environmental, and political concerns. The training that planners receive serves them well in many types of employment situations.

At times, planners work with every other environmental manager discussed in this book, most frequently with architects, geographers, and landscape architects. And they work with government officials and politicians.

Planners increasingly are becoming involved in social issues such as the housing needs of minorities and diverse cultures, an aging population, housing and treatment facilities for people with AIDS, shelters for the homeless, and drug treatment centers. Planners work closely with those of the ancillary professions, including—in the cases just cited—social workers, physicians, elective officials, city managers, lawyers, and civic activists and advocates, such as those working with the homeless and people with AIDS.

How frequently planners meet such special circumstances depends on where they work, and it would be most frequent in urban areas. More commonly, planners spend their time examining universal community needs such as for schools, libraries, and health clinics, and the necessities and amenities of modern life: office buildings and industrial parks, shopping malls, transportation, roads, parking facilities, commuting travel patterns and loads, historic preservation and restoration, downtown restoration and reuse, parks and recreation areas, and pathways and bicycle paths. They must consider economic and legal issues and the environmental impacts of such development.

Inherent in much environmental change is conflict, along with social considerations and economic consequences—usually, somebody loses and somebody wins. The planner is in the middle of some community disputes and often must facilitate resolution of the conflict. This can either be accomplished informally or by more formal conciliation, arbitration, or mediation.

Environmental mediation is an important new adjunct profession in environmental management, and the planner frequently plays a key role as a mediator. The planner also may have to testify before hearing boards and political bodies, participate in public forums and community meetings, and give interviews to radio, television, and newspaper journalists.

The range of such conflicts and the challenge to the planner are suggested by a recent issue of the APA monthly journal *Planning*. It features articles on how the U.S. Department of Housing and Urban Development is responding to the disastrous national housing fraud scandal that was uncovered there in the late 1980s, annexation battles, the planning profession's code of ethics, and environmental law, as well as how public bodies are acquiring inner-city religious buildings (when the congregations move to the suburbs and want to sell them, or their members grow old and the congregations disappear), preserving, renovating, and converting them to everything from housing to community centers to theaters.

What Education Would You Need to Become a Planner?

A few bachelor's programs in planning are offered, but the master's degree is the usual requirement for entry to professional practice. Approximately seventy-five U.S. and two Canadian universities offer a master's degree in urban or regional planning, normally in a two-year program. These programs are accepted by the Planning Accreditation Board, sponsored by the American Institute of Certified Planners and the Association of Collegiate Schools of Planning, both of which are affiliated with APA. Electives generally include demography, economics, finance, healthy administration, location theory, and management.

The bachelor's in planning, or in architecture, architectural history, engineering, or environmental studies, may qualify one for a beginning position in urban and regional planning. Often, work toward the master's can be pursued part-time.

Where Would You Work as a Planner?

Most planners work for city, county, or regional planning agencies. The number of professionals in private business and research organizations is increasing, however. Planners also work for banks, other savings institutions, airline companies, utilities, and other firms that provide services to urban and rural areas, especially when they are subject to governmental regulation.

While the planning field, more and more, is stressing professionalism, still it is general enough to provide many entry-level jobs for environmentalists who might find a general environmental studies education qualifying. Planners are specified in some ads in all the jobs newsletters listed in Chapter 3.

Advertised there and elsewhere are even more openings for which planners might qualify. These openings might be listed as analyst, ombudsman, trainer, information and education specialist, teacher, technical publications editor, or environmental educator.

Overseas, planners work for the Agency for International Development (AID), the World Bank, engineering and consulting firms, and the governments of developing nations.

What Do Planners Earn?

According to a 1987 survey by the APA, urban and regional planners earned a median annual salary of about $36,000—a little less in city governments, much less in county governments; more in state governments, a little more in private consulting firms, and a lot more in business firms. One can assume about a 3 percent rise per year in each category.

The U.S. Office of Personnel Management confirms that planners are hired, when suitable openings are announced, at the starting-level grade of GS-5 with a salary of $16,875. Mid-level positions frequently are at the GS-12/13 levels, with a range of $37,000 to $44,000 to start.

Every week metropolitan newspapers such as the *Washington Post,* the *New York Times,* and the *Los Angeles Times* carry classified advertising for planners, usually specifying a specialty: environmental/natural resources, neighborhood, parks, trails, transportation, etc. All the salary ranges mentioned above are included—from hourly rates as low as $5 for summer and temporary work, to responsible management positions at $60,000 per annum and greater.

What Is the Job Future for Planners?

The Bureau of Labor Statistics estimates present employment at twenty thousand and forecasts a 15 percent increase, which would add three thousand positions by the turn of the century.

Increases can be expected in jobs related to environmental planning, transportation, and energy production, "especially in states that have mandated planning," according to BLS.

Graduates can turn to their advantage the broad, general nature of the field in that the skills are applicable to planning almost anything: strategic planning for implementation of the Clean Air Act Amendments, military operations anywhere in the world, or introduction and marketing of any new consumer product.

WHERE SHOULD YOU WRITE FOR MORE INFORMATION?

American Institute of Architects
1735 New York Avenue, N.W.
Washington, D.C. 20006

American Planning Association
1776 Massachusetts Avenue, N.W.
Washington, D.C. 20036

American Society of Landscape Architects
4401 Connecticut Avenue, N.W.
Washington, D.C. 20008-2302

Association of American Geographers
1710 16th Street, N.W.
Washington, D.C. 20009

National Geographic Society
Geography Education Program
17th and M Streets, N.W.
Washington, D.C. 20036

CHAPTER 7

TOMORROW'S NEW ENVIRONMENTALISM

   The 1990s must clearly be committed to protecting our global environment. I predict that during this decade, the "Decade of the Environment," we will see—across this nation and around the world—a social movement that in terms of impact will exceed the civil rights movement within this country or the pro-democracy movement in Europe. Because fundamental to the values represented by these important movements is the essential commitment to environmental justice. It is impossible to enjoy our human rights and freedoms except in the context of a healthy environment.—Jay D. Hair, Ph.D., president and chief executive officer, National Wildlife Federation, in Earth Day address, April 21, 1990, National Museum of Natural History, the Smithsonian Institution, Washington, D.C.

Dr. Hair made the statement above before the United States went to war against Iraq in January 1991. The BLS traditionally has predicated its predictions on the assumption that "No major event such as war or widespread or long-lasting energy shortages will significantly alter the industrial structure of the economy or the rate of economic growth." (War in the Persian Gulf region also could result in energy shortages and higher energy prices throughout the world.)

War effectively nullifies all assumptions regarding gross national product, economic output, productivity, inflation, defense spending, consumer spending, energy supply and prices, taxes, and every other facet of the economy. And it inevitably brings unemployment in many sectors and many regions of the country.

Environmental professions are not generally subject to as much uncertainty as are those in retail and consumer businesses, banking, the stock market, and other sectors. Major federal and private sector programs are planned and funded at least a year in advance. Moreover, many large programs—Superfund is an example—have been mandated by law and will continue, perhaps with reduced but still large appropriations, regardless of the impact of events such as war.

War becomes just one factor; equally great consequences are being felt from the federal budget deficit, the savings-and-loan scandal, and the stagnant growth of the economy. State and local governments, which under other conditions might have taken up the slack in federal programs, are themselves experiencing great deficits. Because of the war effort, the deficit is growing; taxes may have to be raised.

What about tomorrow? For the same reasons that the environmental field has grown so rapidly over the past two decades, we can be optimistic that environmental programs will be especially favored among all domestic programs as soon as peace is restored.

Meanwhile, environmental programs must be staffed and retirees replaced. The BLS has developed a theory about the significance of generational turnover and the significance of replacements, especially in a rapidly growing field. The *Occupational Outlook Handbook* explains:

> Replacement openings occur as people leave occupations. Some individuals transfer to other occupations as a step up the career ladder or to change careers. Some stop working temporarily, perhaps to return to school or [to] care for a family. And some leave the labor force permanently—retirees, for example. In most occupations, replacement needs provide more job openings than does growth.

As shown in the preface to this book, in the first generation of the environmental era, roughly from 1970 to 1990, professional jobs in environmental management more than doubled, from half a million to more than a million; depending upon how one delineates the field, it could be up to twice as large. We call these the *new environmentalists.* Today, many of those practitioners are retiring and are being replaced; it is a large field experiencing extensive work force turnover. From now until early in the next century, we will be in the second generation of environmental management.

Most of this generation, as the preface notes, were not even born at the time of the first Earth Day in 1970 and were still in secondary school at the time of the twentieth in 1990. Come the year 2010, most of this generation should be stepping aside, making way for a third generation of new environmentalists.

Dr. Hair addresses *values* and *environmental justice,* two concepts which should not be lost sight of in peacetime or wartime. War wreaks havoc on the human environment. Peace brings the opportunity to repair war's damages, to rebuild international relationships, and hopefully to restore human rights and freedoms for all peoples, in the context of a healthy environment for all.

This is the future which should provide bright prospects for opportunities in environmental and other careers.

APPENDIX A

CITIZEN ORGANIZATIONS

(Not previously listed)

The American Forestry Association, 1516 P Street, N.W., Washington, D.C. 20005. Publication: *American Forests*

American Land Resource Association, 5410 Grosvenor Lane, Bethesda, Md. 20814

The American Museum of Natural History, Central Park West at 79th Street, New York, N.Y. 10024. Publication: *Natural History Magazine*

The Cousteau Society, 930 West 21st Street, Norfolk, Va. 23517. Publication: *Calypso Log*

Defenders of Wildlife, 1244 19th Street, N.W., Washington, D.C. 20036. Publication: *Defenders*

Environmental Action, 1525 New Hampshire Avenue, N.W., Washington, D.C. 20036. Publication: *Environmental Action*

Environmental Defense Fund, 444 Park Avenue South, New York, N.Y. 10016. Publication: *EDF Letter*

Environmental Task Force, 1525 New Hampshire Avenue, N.W., Washington, D.C. 20036. Publication: *Re:Sources*

Friends of the Earth, 1045 Sansome Street, San Francisco, Calif. 94111. Publication: *Not Man Apart*

Greenpeace USA, 1436 U Street, N.W., Washington, D.C. 20009. Publication: *Greenpeace Magazine*

Human Environment Center, 1001 Connecticut Avenue, N.W., Washington, D.C. 20036

The Izaak Walton League of America, 1401 Wilson Boulevard, Arlington, Va. 22209. Publication: *Outdoor America*

League of Conservation Voters, 1150 Connecticut Avenue, N.W., Washington, D.C. 20036

National Audubon Society, 950 Third Avenue, New York, N.Y. 10022. Publication: *Audubon*

National Geographic Society, 17th and M Streets, N.W., Washington, D.C. 20036. Publication: *National Geographic*

National Parks & Conservation Association, 1015 31st Street, N.W., Washington, D.C. 20007. Publication: *National Parks & Conservation Magazine*

National Trust for Historic Preservation, 1785 Massachusetts Avenue, N.W., Washington, D.C. 20036. Publication: *Historic Preservation*

Natural Resources Defense Council, 122 East 42nd Street, New York, N.Y. 10017. Publication: *The Amicus Journal*

The Nature Conservancy, 1815 North Lynn Street, Arlington, Va. 22209. Publication: *Nature Conservancy*

Population-Environment Balance, 1325 G Street, N.W., Suite 1003, Washington, D.C. 20005. Publication: *Balance Report*

Rachel Carson Council, 8940 Jones Mill Road, Washington, D.C. 20815.

Sierra Club, 730 Polk Street, San Francisco, Calif. 94109. Publication: *Sierra*

Smithsonian Institution, 1000 Jefferson Drive, S.W., Washington, D.C. 20560. Publication: *Smithsonian*

The Wilderness Society, 1401 Eye Street, N.W., Washington, D.C. 20005. Publication: *The Living Wilderness*

Zero Population Growth, 1400 16th Street, N.W., Washington, D.C. 20036

KEY FEDERAL AGENCIES

ACTION, Washington, D.C. 20525
  Peace Corps, VISTA
Department of Agriculture, Washington, D.C. 20250
  Forest Service; Science and Education Administration; Soil Conservation
  Service
Department of Commerce, Washington, D.C. 20230
  National Oceanic and Atmospheric Administration, Rockville, Md. 20852
Congress of the United States, Washington, D.C. 20510
  Office of Technology Assessment
Consumer Product Safety Commission, Washington, D.C. 20207
Council on Environmental Quality, Washington, D.C. 20006
Department of Defense, Washington, D.C. 20301
Department of Education, Washington, D.C. 20202
Department of Energy, Washington, D.C. 20585
Environment Canada, Ottawa, Ontario, Canada K1A OH3
Environmental Protection Agency, Washington, D.C. 20460
  Environmental Research Center, National Training and Operational
  Technology Center, Cincinnati, Ohio 45268
  Environmental Research Laboratory, Research Triangle Park, N.C. 22709
Federal Emergency Management Agency, Washington, D.C. 20472
Department of Health and Human Services, Washington, D.C. 20201
  Centers for Disease Control, Atlanta, Ga. 30333
  National Institute for Occupational Safety and Health, Rockville, Md. 20857
  Food and Drug Administration, Rockville, Md. 20857
  National Institutes of Health, Bethesda, Md. 20205
  National Institute of Environmental Health Sciences, Research Triangle Park,
  N.C. 22709

Department of Housing and Urban Development, Washington, D.C. 20410
Department of the Interior, Washington, D.C. 20240
   Fish and Wildlife Service
   National Park Service
Department of Labor, Washington, D.C. 20210
   Bureau of Labor Statistics; Occupational Safety and Health Administration
National Aeronautics and Space Administration, Washington, D.C. 20546
National Science Foundation, Washington, D.C. 20550
Nuclear Regulatory Commission, Washington, D.C. 20555
Smithsonian Institution, Washington, D.C. 20560
Department of Transportation, Washington, D.C. 20590
Veterans Administration, Washington, D.C. 20420

VGM CAREER BOOKS

OPPORTUNITIES IN
Available in both paperback and hardbound editions
Accounting
Acting
Advertising
Aerospace
Agriculture
Airline
Animal and Pet Care
Architecture
Automotive Service
Banking
Beauty Culture
Biological Sciences
Biotechnology
Book Publishing
Broadcasting
Building Construction Trades
Business Communication
Business Management
Cable Television
Carpentry
Chemical Engineering
Chemistry
Child Care
Chiropractic Health Care
Civil Engineering
Cleaning Service
Commercial Art and Graphic Design
Computer Aided Design and
    Computer Aided Mfg.
Computer Maintenance
Computer Science
Counseling & Development
Crafts
Culinary
Customer Service
Dance
Data Processing
Dental Care
Direct Marketing
Drafting
Electrical Trades
Electronic and Electrical Engineering
Electronics
Energy
Engineering
Engineering Technology
Environmental
Eye Care
Fashion
Fast Food
Federal Government
Film
Financial
Fire Protection Services
Fitness
Food Services
Foreign Language
Forestry
Gerontology
Government Service
Graphic Communications
Health and Medical
High Tech
Home Economics
Hospital Administration
Hotel & Motel Management
Human Resources Management
    Careers
Information Systems
Insurance
Interior Design
International Business
Journalism
Laser Technology
Law

Law Enforcement and Criminal Justice
Library and Information Science
Machine Trades
Magazine Publishing
Management
Marine & Maritime
Marketing
Materials Science
Mechanical Engineering
Medical Technology
Metalworking
Microelectronics
Military
Modeling
Music
Newspaper Publishing
Nursing
Nutrition
Occupational Therapy
Office Occupations
Opticianry
Optometry
Packaging Science
Paralegal Careers
Paramedical Careers
Part-time & Summer Jobs
Performing Arts
Petroleum
Pharmacy
Photography
Physical Therapy
Physician
Plastics
Plumbing & Pipe Fitting
Podiatric Medicine
Postal Service
Printing
Property Management
Psychiatry
Psychology
Public Health
Public Relations
Purchasing
Real Estate
Recreation and Leisure
Refrigeration and Air Conditioning
Religious Service
Restaurant
Retailing
Robotics
Sales
Sales & Marketing
Secretarial
Securities
Social Science
Social Work
Speech-Language Pathology
Sports & Athletics
Sports Medicine
State and Local Government
Teaching
Technical Communications
Telecommunications
Television and Video
Theatrical Design & Production
Transportation
Travel
Trucking
Veterinary Medicine
Visual Arts
Vocational and Technical
Warehousing
Waste Management
Welding
Word Processing
Writing
Your Own Service Business

CAREERS IN Accounting; Advertising;
Business; Communications; Computers;
Education; Engineering; Health Care;
High Tech; Law; Marketing; Medicine;
Science

CAREER DIRECTORIES
Careers Encyclopedia
Dictionary of Occupational Titles
Occupational Outlook Handbook

CAREER PLANNING
Admissions Guide to Selective
    Business Schools
Career Planning and Development for
    College Students and Recent
    Graduates
Careers Checklists
Careers for Animal Lovers
Careers for Bookworms
Careers for Culture Lovers
Careers for Foreign Language
    Aficionados
Careers for Good Samaritans
Careers for Gourmets
Careers for Nature Lovers
Careers for Numbers Crunchers
Careers for Sports Nuts
Careers for Travel Buffs
Guide to Basic Resume Writing
Handbook of Business and
    Management Careers
Handbook of Health Care Careers
Handbook of Scientific and
    Technical Careers
How to Change Your Career
How to Choose the Right Career
How to Get and Keep
    Your First Job
How to Get into the Right Law School
How to Get People to Do Things
    Your Way
How to Have a Winning Job Interview
How to Land a Better Job
How to Make the Right Career Moves
How to Market Your College Degree
How to Prepare a *Curriculum Vitae*
How to Prepare for College
How to Run Your Own Home Business
How to Succeed in Collge
How to Succeed in High School
How to Write a Winning Resume
Joyce Lain Kennedy's Career Book
Planning Your Career of Tomorrow
Planning Your College Education
Planning Your Military Career
Planning Your Young Child's
    Education
Resumes for Advertising Careers
Resumes for College Students & Recent
    Graduates
Resumes for Communications Careers
Resumes for Education Careers
Resumes for High School Graduates
Resumes for High Tech Careers
Resumes for Sales and Marketing Careers
Successful Interviewing for College
    Seniors

SURVIVAL GUIDES
Dropping Out or Hanging In
High School Survival Guide
College Survival Guide

VGM Career Horizons
a division of *NTC Publishing Group*
4255 West Touhy Avenue
Lincolnwood, Illinois 60646-1975